THE FUTURE OF DATA SCIENCE: TRENDS AND TECHNOLOGIES SHAPING THE FIELD

M.RAMPRASATH

Contents

ONE
INTRODUCTION

The world is awash in data. Every day, we generate exabytes of information from our smartphones, social media interactions, online transactions, and countless other sources. This data deluge, often referred to as "big data," presents both challenges and opportunities for businesses, organizations, and individuals. The future of data science is a dynamic landscape, shaped by the convergence of exponential data growth, advanced algorithms, and emerging technologies. From the depths of artificial intelligence and machine learning to the vast expanse of big data analytics, data scientists are at the forefront of innovation. As industries across the globe become increasingly data-driven, the demand for skilled professionals who can extract meaningful insights from complex datasets will continue to soar. This book delves into the trends and technologies that are revolutionizing the field, exploring their implications for businesses, society, and the data scientists themselves.Trends and Technologies Shaping the Field encapsulates the dynamic and transformative nature of a discipline rapidly reshaping industries and societies. This book delves into the core of this revolution, exploring the cutting-edge technologies that are driving data-driven innovation. It examines how the exponential growth of data is being harnessed to extract unprecedented insights, and how these insights are being translated into tangible business value. Data science is the interdisciplinary field that extracts knowledge and insights from structured and unstructured data through scientific methods, algorithms, and systems. It is a fusion of statistics, computer science, and domain expertise, enabling organizations to make informed decisions, optimize processes, and uncover hidden patterns. From finance and healthcare to marketing and retail, data science has become an indispensable tool for driving innovation and gaining a competitive edge in today's data-driven world. This powerful discipline combines elements of statistics, mathematics, computer science, and domain expertise to uncover hidden patterns, trends, and correlations. By harnessing the potential of vast datasets, data scientists drive innovation, inform strategic decision-making, and create new opportunities across industries, from healthcare and finance to marketing and beyond.Data science is the art and science of extracting valuable insights from vast and complex datasets. It is an interdisciplinary field that blends statistics, computer science, and domain expertise to uncover hidden patterns, trends, and correlations. With the exponential growth of data generated across industries, data science has emerged as a critical driver of innovation and decision-making. By harnessing the power of data, organizations can optimize operations, identify new opportunities, and gain a competitive edge in today's data-driven world.The landscape of data science is in a state of constant evolution, driven by a confluence of emerging technologies and rapidly changing trends. From the foundational pillars of artificial intelligence and machine learning to the transformative potential of big data analytics, the field is experiencing unprecedented growth. This dynamic interplay between technological advancements and evolving industry demands is reshaping how organizations extract value from their data, driving innovation and creating new opportunities across sectors. From the exponential growth of data to the sophistication of artificial intelligence, the field is experiencing a paradigm shift. This book delves into the heart of these developments, examining how advancements in technology are reshaping the way organizations capture, process, and leverage data. By understanding the trends and technologies driving this transformation, readers will gain valuable insights into the future of data science and its potential impact on various industries. We live in an age defined by data. From the moment we wake up to the time we go to sleep, we generate vast quantities of information that is reshaping industries, societies, and our very understanding of the world. At the heart of this data revolution lies data science, a discipline that transforms raw information into actionable insights.

This book, The Future of Data Science: Trends and Technologies Shaping the Field, is a comprehensive exploration of the forces driving this dynamic field. We delve into the core technologies propelling data science forward, examining how artificial intelligence, machine learning, and big data analytics are redefining possibilities. Furthermore, we explore how these advancements are being applied across diverse industries, from healthcare and finance to marketing and beyond. Beyond the technical aspects, we also consider the broader implications of data science. As this field matures, it raises critical questions about ethics, privacy, and the future of work. By understanding the trends and challenges shaping data science, we can better prepare for the opportunities and responsibilities that lie ahead.

TWO
THE DATA REVOLUTION

The Data Revolution is reshaping the world around us. An unprecedented surge in data generation, fueled by the proliferation of digital devices and online activities, has created a wealth of information that holds immense potential. From businesses seeking to optimize operations to governments aiming to improve public services, organizations across sectors are recognizing the power of data to drive innovation and decision-making. As we delve into the intricacies of this data-driven landscape, we will explore how data is being harnessed to unlock new opportunities and address complex challenges. The relentless march of technological advancement has ushered in an era defined by data. From the sprawling metropolis to the tranquil countryside, data is being generated at an unprecedented rate. Businesses, governments, and individuals alike are grappling with the immense potential and complexities of this digital deluge. As data volumes continue to explode, so too does the demand for skilled professionals capable of transforming raw information into actionable insights. Data science, at the intersection of statistics, computer science, and domain expertise, has emerged as the linchpin in this data-driven revolution. By harnessing the power of advanced algorithms and sophisticated analytical tools, data scientists are unlocking hidden patterns, predicting future trends, and optimizing processes across industries. Billions of interconnected devices, from smartphones to industrial sensors, generate an overwhelming torrent of information every second. This data deluge presents both immense challenges and extraordinary opportunities. Organizations that can effectively harness and analyze these vast datasets are poised to gain a competitive advantage. From optimizing business operations and predicting customer behavior to developing life-saving medical treatments and addressing global challenges, the potential applications of data science are boundless. As we navigate this complex landscape, it is imperative to understand the underlying trends and technologies that are shaping the future of data science. By exploring the intersection of artificial intelligence, machine learning, big data analytics, and emerging domains like the Internet of Things, we can unlock the full potential of data and drive innovation across industries.

The are living in the midst of a data deluge. The digital revolution has unleashed an unprecedented torrent of information, generated at a pace that defies comprehension. From the mundane to the monumental, data is being created at every turn. Social media platforms capture our likes, shares, and comments. Online transactions leave a digital footprint. Sensors embedded in everything from smartphones to industrial equipment generate vast quantities of data. This exponential growth has transformed data from a mere resource into a strategic asset. The implications of this data explosion are far-reaching. Businesses are leveraging it to gain insights into customer behavior, optimize operations, and develop new products. Governments are using data to improve public services and make informed policy decisions. Even individuals are harnessing the power of data to manage their personal lives more effectively. However, the sheer volume and complexity of this data pose significant challenges. The contemporary world is inundated with data, a relentless deluge that shows no signs of abating. This phenomenon, often termed the "data explosion," is a direct consequence of the rapid advancements in technology and the increasing interconnectedness of our digital lives.

At the heart of this data deluge is the proliferation of digital devices. Smartphones, tablets, and laptops have become ubiquitous, generating vast quantities of data through user interactions, app usage, and internet browsing. Social media platforms, with their billions of active users, contribute significantly to this data explosion, as every like, share, comment, and post adds to the growing volume of information.

Beyond personal devices, the Internet of Things (IoT) is a major driver of data growth. Billions of connected devices, from smart homes to industrial sensors, are constantly collecting and transmitting data about their environment. This data, often referred to as machine-generated data, provides invaluable insights into various systems and processes.

The implications of this data explosion are profound. Businesses are leveraging it to gain a competitive edge, governments are using it to improve public services, and researchers are using it to make groundbreaking discoveries. However, the sheer volume and complexity of this data present significant challenges. To harness its full potential, organizations must develop sophisticated data management and analysis capabilities.

In essence, the data explosion is a double-edged sword. On the one hand, it offers unprecedented opportunities for innovation and growth. On the other hand, it demands new approaches to data storage, processing, and security. As we delve deeper into the digital age, managing and extracting value from this tidal wave of information will be a critical challenge for individuals, businesses, and societies alike.

THE RISE OF BIG DATA

The term "big data" encapsulates the massive and complex datasets that traditional data-processing applications struggle to manage efficiently. This phenomenon has emerged as a direct consequence of the digital revolution, which has led to an exponential growth in data generation. The advent of the internet, coupled with the proliferation of digital devices, has created an unprecedented volume of data. Social media platforms, e-commerce websites, and online streaming services generate vast amounts of information about user behavior, preferences, and interactions. Additionally, the Internet of Things (IoT) has contributed significantly to the big data phenomenon, as billions of connected devices collect and transmit data about their surroundings Big data is characterized by its three Vs:

- **Volume:** The sheer quantity of data generated is immense, often measured in petabytes or even exabytes.
- **Velocity:** Data is generated and processed at an increasingly rapid pace, requiring real-time analysis capabilities.
- **Variety:** Big data encompasses a wide range of data types, including structured, unstructured, and semi-structured data, such as text, images, videos, and sensor data.

The rise of big data has presented both challenges and opportunities. On one hand, it offers the potential to extract valuable insights and make data-driven decisions. On the other hand, managing and processing such large and complex datasets requires advanced technologies and skilled professionals. As organizations continue to grapple with the complexities of big data, it is clear that it will play a pivotal role in shaping the future of business, government, and society.

Applications of Big Data Across Different Industries

Big data has revolutionized how businesses operate across various sectors. Here are some key applications:

Healthcare:

- Personalized medicine: Analyzing patient data to tailor treatments.
- Disease outbreak prediction: Identifying patterns in health data to anticipate epidemics.

- Drug discovery: Accelerating the research process by analyzing vast datasets.

Finance:

- Fraud detection: Identifying anomalies in financial transactions.
- Risk assessment: Evaluating investment opportunities and creditworthiness.
- Customer segmentation: Tailoring financial products to specific customer groups.

Marketing:

- Customer segmentation: Grouping customers based on behavior and preferences.
- Targeted advertising: Delivering relevant ads to specific audiences.
- Customer churn prediction: Identifying customers likely to leave a company.

Retail:

- Inventory management: Optimizing stock levels based on demand patterns.
- Customer behavior analysis: Understanding shopping habits to enhance the customer experience.
- Supply chain optimization: Improving efficiency and reducing costs.

Challenges in Managing Big Data

Despite its potential, big data presents numerous challenges:

- **Data Quality:** Ensuring data accuracy, completeness, and consistency is crucial.

- **Data Storage:** Storing massive datasets requires efficient and scalable storage solutions.
- **Data Processing:** Analyzing large volumes of data demands powerful computing resources.
- **Data Security:** Protecting sensitive data from unauthorized access is paramount.
- **Data Privacy:** Complying with data privacy regulations is essential.
- **Data Integration:** Combining data from various sources can be complex.
- **Talent Shortage:** Finding skilled professionals to manage big data is challenging.

Technologies for Processing and Analyzing Big Data

To overcome these challenges, organizations employ a range of technologies:

- **Hadoop:** An open-source framework for storing and processing large datasets across clusters of computers.
- **Spark:** A fast and general-purpose cluster computing framework for big data processing.
- **NoSQL Databases:** Designed to handle large volumes of unstructured or semi-structured data.
- **Data Warehouses:** Centralized repositories for structured data, optimized for querying and analysis.
- **Data Lakes:** Storage repositories that hold a variety of raw data in its native format.
- **Cloud Computing:** Provides scalable computing resources for big data processing.
- **Machine Learning:** Algorithms to extract patterns and insights from large datasets.

By effectively addressing these challenges and leveraging appropriate technologies, organizations can unlock the full potential of big data and gain a competitive advantage.

DATA LAKES AND DATA WAREHOUSES

Data lakes and data warehouses are essential components of modern data management strategies, each serving distinct purposes within an organization's data architecture.

Data Lakes

A data lake is a centralized repository that stores raw data in its native format. It acts as a vast, unstructured reservoir for data from various sources, including structured, semi-structured, and unstructured data. Think of it as a digital dumping ground where data is collected without predefined schema or structure.

Key characteristics of data lakes:

- **Schema-on-read:** The structure of data is defined when it's queried, allowing for flexibility and adaptability.
- **Variety:** Accommodates diverse data types, including text, images, videos, and sensor data.
- **Velocity:** Can handle high-velocity data ingestion.
- **Volume:** Scalable to store massive amounts of data.
- **Cost-effective:** Typically cheaper to store data in its raw format.

Data lakes are ideal for exploratory data analysis, data science projects, and machine learning initiatives where the exact use cases for the data may not be defined upfront.

Data Warehouses

A data warehouse is a centralized repository of structured data that has been cleaned, transformed, and integrated for analysis and reporting. It's designed to provide a single version of the truth for business intelligence and decision-making.

Key characteristics of data warehouses:

- **Schema-on-write:** Data is structured and organized during the loading process.
- **Structured data:** Primarily stores structured data for efficient querying.

- **Performance-optimized**: Designed for fast query performance and reporting.
- **Business-focused**: Aligned with specific business requirements and reporting needs.

Data warehouses are suitable for producing standardized reports, dashboards, and business intelligence insights.

Challenges in Managing Data Lakes

- Data Quality: Ensuring data accuracy, consistency, and completeness in a vast, unstructured environment is complex.
- Data Governance: Establishing clear ownership, access controls, and data retention policies is crucial but challenging.
- Metadata Management: Effectively managing metadata to understand data content and lineage is essential.
- Security and Privacy: Protecting sensitive data in a data lake requires robust security measures.
- Performance: Querying unstructured data can be slow and inefficient without proper optimization.

Challenges in Managing Data Warehouses

- Data Integration: Combining data from various sources into a consistent format can be time-consuming and error-prone.
- Data Latency: Maintaining up-to-date data in a data warehouse can be challenging, especially for rapidly changing data.
- Scalability: Expanding a data warehouse to accommodate growing data volumes can be costly and complex.
- Data Volume: Handling large volumes of data efficiently can be resource-intensive.
- Cost: Building and maintaining a data warehouse can be expensive.

DATA DEMOCRATIZATION

Data democratization is the process of making data accessible and understandable to everyone within an organization, regardless of their technical expertise.

It's about breaking down data silos, providing the right tools, and fostering a data-driven culture where insights drive decisions at all levels.

The Core Idea

Traditionally, data has been a domain reserved for data scientists and analysts. However, in today's data-driven world, this approach is no longer sufficient. Data democratization aims to:

Expand Data Access

Breaking down data silos: Traditionally, data has been confined to IT or analytics departments. To maximize its value, organizations must democratize data access. This involves:

- Centralized data repositories: Consolidating data from various sources into a single, accessible location.
- Data catalogs: Creating comprehensive inventories of available data, including metadata and usage guidelines.
- Role-based access controls: Ensuring data security by granting appropriate permissions to different user groups.
- Self-service data preparation: Empowering users to clean, transform, and prepare data for analysis without relying solely on IT.

Simplify Data Consumption

To make data accessible to everyone, regardless of technical expertise, organizations should:

- User-friendly interfaces: Developing intuitive dashboards and visualizations that present complex data in easily understandable formats.
- Natural language processing: Enabling users to interact with data using everyday language through conversational interfaces.

- Automated insights: Leveraging AI and machine learning to generate actionable insights and recommendations.
- Data storytelling: Transforming data into compelling narratives that resonate with different audiences.

Promote Data Literacy

Investing in data literacy is crucial for a data-driven culture. This involves:

- Data literacy training: Providing employees with the skills to understand, interpret, and analyze data effectively.
- Data visualization workshops: Teaching employees how to create impactful visuals to communicate data insights.
- Mentorship programs: Pairing data experts with less experienced employees to foster knowledge sharing.
- Data challenges and competitions: Encouraging a playful approach to data exploration and analysis.

Foster a Data-Driven Culture

A data-driven culture is characterized by a shared belief in the power of data to inform decision-making. To cultivate this culture:

- Leadership buy-in: Demonstrating top-level support for data initiatives and setting clear expectations.
- Data-driven decision-making: Encouraging employees to use data to support their recommendations and actions.
- Data-centric rewards: Recognizing and rewarding employees who effectively leverage data to achieve business goals.
- Data-focused communication: Integrating data into regular business conversations and reports.
- Change management: Addressing resistance to change and providing support during the transition to a data-driven culture.

By implementing these strategies, organizations can unlock the full potential of their data, drive innovation, improve decision-making, and gain a competitive advantage.

Benefits of Data Democratization

- Faster decision-making: Employees can access and analyze data quickly, leading to faster and more informed decisions.
- Improved agility: Organizations can respond to market changes and opportunities more rapidly.
- Enhanced innovation: A data-driven culture encourages experimentation and new ideas.
- Increased efficiency: Automating data-driven tasks can free up time for employees to focus on higher-value activities.
- Better customer experience: Data-driven insights can help organizations understand customer needs and preferences better.

Key Components of Data Democratization

1. **Data Accessibility:**

   - Centralized data repositories: Make data easily accessible from a single location.
   - Data catalogs: Provide clear documentation and metadata about data assets.
   - Self-service data preparation: Empower users to clean and transform data without relying on IT.

2. **Data Literacy:**

   - Data literacy training: Equip employees with the skills to understand, analyze, and communicate data effectively.
   - Data storytelling: Teach employees how to present data insights in a compelling and engaging way.
   - Data visualization: Provide tools for creating visual representations of data.

3. **Data Governance:**

   - Data quality: Ensure data accuracy, consistency, and reliability.
   - Data security: Protect sensitive data from unauthorized access.
   - Data privacy: Comply with data protection regulations.

4. **Data Culture:**

   - Data-driven mindset: Foster a culture where data is valued and used for decision-making.
   - Data champions: Identify and empower employees who can lead data initiatives.
   - Data collaboration: Encourage cross-functional teams to work together on data projects.

Challenges and Considerations

- **Data overload:** Too much data can be overwhelming. Prioritize data and focus on what's essential.
- **Data security:** Protect sensitive data while ensuring accessibility.
- **Data quality:** Ensure data accuracy and consistency to avoid misleading insights.
- **Change management:** Overcoming resistance to change and building buy-in for data democratization.

Examples of Data Democratization in Action

- **Sales teams** using data to identify sales opportunities and optimize sales processes.
- **Marketing teams** leveraging customer data to personalize campaigns and improve customer engagement.
- **Operations teams** using data to optimize supply chain and inventory management.

- **HR teams** using data to analyze employee performance and identify talent gaps.

By empowering everyone in the organization with data, companies can unlock its full potential, drive innovation, and gain a competitive advantage.

DATA GOVERNANCE AND QUALITY

Data governance and data quality are two interconnected pillars that underpin the reliability and value of an organization's data. Together, they ensure that data is accurate, complete, consistent, relevant, and timely, fostering trust and confidence in decision-making.

Data Governance

Data governance is the overall management of the availability, usability, integrity, and security of the data employed in an enterprise. It involves establishing standards, policies, and procedures to ensure data is used effectively and responsibly.

Key components of data governance include:

- **Data ownership:** Defining who is responsible for specific data assets.
- **Data stewardship:** Assigning individuals to oversee data quality and usage.
- **Data policies:** Creating guidelines for data collection, storage, usage, and retention.
- **Data standards:** Establishing consistent formats, definitions, and metadata.
- **Data security:** Implementing measures to protect data from unauthorized access and breaches.
- **Data compliance:** Adhering to relevant regulations and industry standards (e.g., GDPR, HIPAA).
- **Data quality management:** Incorporating data quality as a core component of governance.

Data Quality

Data quality focuses on the accuracy, completeness, consistency, relevance, and timeliness of data. It ensures that data is fit for its intended use.

Key dimensions of data quality include:

- **Accuracy:** Data is correct and free from errors.
- **Completeness:** Data is complete and contains all necessary information.
- **Consistency:** Data is consistent across different sources and formats.
- **Relevance:** Data is relevant to the intended purpose.
- **Timeliness:** Data is up-to-date and available when needed.

The Interplay Between Data Governance and Data Quality

Data governance provides the framework for managing data quality. It establishes the roles, responsibilities, and processes necessary to maintain high data quality standards. Conversely, data quality is a critical component of data governance, as

By effectively combining data governance and data quality initiatives, organizations can:

- **Improve decision-making:** By relying on accurate and complete data.
- **Enhance operational efficiency:** By streamlining data processes and reducing errors.
- **Mitigate risks:** By ensuring data compliance and security.
- **Build trust:** By demonstrating a commitment to data integrity.

In essence, data governance and data quality are essential for creating a data-driven culture where information is trusted and leveraged to achieve organizational goals.

Challenges

- Data Quality Issues: How to identify and address data inconsistencies, inaccuracies, and incompleteness.

- Data Governance Implementation: Overcoming resistance to change, defining roles and responsibilities, and establishing a governance framework.
- Balancing Data Accessibility and Security: Protecting sensitive data while ensuring it's available for analysis.
- Data Lineage and Provenance: Tracking data from source to consumption for accountability and compliance.

Strategies

- Data Profiling and Cleansing: Techniques for improving data quality.
- Data Catalog and Metadata Management: Creating a centralized repository of data assets.
- Data Democratization: Empowering business users while maintaining control.
- Data Governance Tools and Technologies: Leveraging technology to streamline processes.

DATA SECURITY AND PRIVACY OF PROTECTING SENSITIVE INFORMATION

Data security and privacy have become paramount in today's digital age. As organizations increasingly collect, store, and process sensitive information, the risks of data breaches and privacy violations have grown exponentially. This section delves into the critical aspects of protecting sensitive information.

Understanding Data Security and Privacy

- **Data Security:** Refers to the technical measures and controls implemented to protect data from unauthorized access, use, disclosure, disruption, modification, or destruction.
- **Data Privacy:** Focuses on the legal and ethical handling of personal information, ensuring individuals have control over their data and that it is processed lawfully and fairly.

Key Components of Data Protection
Risk Assessment:

- Identify potential threats and vulnerabilities to data assets.
- Evaluate the impact of a data breach.
- Prioritize risks based on likelihood and severity.

Data Inventory and Classification:

- Catalog sensitive data assets.
- Classify data based on sensitivity levels (e.g., public, internal, confidential, highly confidential).
- Implement appropriate protection measures based on classification.

Access Controls:

- Implement strong access controls to restrict data access to authorized personnel.
- Employ role-based access control (RBAC) to grant permissions based on job functions.
- Enforce the principle of least privilege, granting only necessary access.

Encryption:

- Protect data at rest and in transit using robust encryption algorithms.
- Consider encryption key management and protection.

Data Loss Prevention (DLP):

- Implement DLP solutions to prevent unauthorized data transfer.

- Monitor and control data movement within and outside the organization.

Network Security:

- Protect the network infrastructure with firewalls, intrusion detection and prevention systems (IDPS), and virtual private networks (VPNs).
- Regularly update security software and patches.

Employee Awareness and Training:

- Educate employees about data security best practices.
- Conduct regular security awareness training to prevent human error.
- Implement policies for handling sensitive information.

Incident Response Plan:

- Develop a comprehensive incident response plan to address data breaches effectively.
- Establish procedures for detection, containment, eradication, recovery, and lessons learned.

Compliance with Regulations:

- Adhere to relevant data protection laws and regulations (e.g., GDPR, CCPA, HIPAA).
- Conduct regular compliance audits and assessments.

Data Retention and Disposal:

- Implement data retention policies to determine data lifecycle.
- Securely dispose of data when no longer needed.

Protecting Sensitive Information

- **Personally Identifiable Information (PII):**

    ◦ Minimize data collection.
    ◦ Obtain explicit consent for data processing.
    ◦ Implement data minimization principles.

- **Payment Card Information (PCI):**

    ◦ Comply with PCI DSS standards.
    ◦ Protect cardholder data with encryption and tokenization.
    ◦ Regularly monitor for vulnerabilities.

- **Intellectual Property:**

    ◦ Safeguard trade secrets and patents.
    ◦ Implement access controls and non-disclosure agreements.
    ◦ Protect against unauthorized disclosure.

Emerging Threats and Challenges

- **Cyberattacks:** Ransomware, phishing, and social engineering attacks pose significant risks.
- **Data Breaches:** The consequences of data breaches can be severe, including financial losses, reputational damage, and legal liabilities.
- **Insider Threats:** Employees can pose risks through accidental or malicious actions.
- **Cloud Security:** Protecting data in cloud environments requires careful consideration of access controls, encryption, and data residency.

By implementing a robust data security and privacy framework, organizations can mitigate risks, protect sensitive information, and build trust with customers and stakeholders.

Data Breaches:

A data breach occurs when sensitive information is accessed by unauthorized individuals. The consequences of a data breach can be catastrophic, leading to financial loss, reputational damage, and legal liabilities.

Types of Data Breaches

- **Accidental Data Loss:** Human error, system failures, or natural disasters can result in data loss.
- **Cyberattacks:** Malicious actors exploit vulnerabilities to steal or damage data. This includes:

  - Phishing: Deceiving users into revealing sensitive information.
  - Malware: Malicious software that infects systems and steals data.
  - Ransomware: Encrypting data and demanding a ransom for decryption.
  - SQL Injection: Exploiting vulnerabilities in web applications.
  - Denial-of-Service (DoS) Attacks: Overwhelming systems to prevent legitimate access.

Impact of Data Breaches

- Financial Loss: Direct costs (incident response, legal fees, regulatory fines), lost revenue, and increased insurance premiums.
- Reputational Damage: Loss of customer trust, negative publicity, and impact on brand value.
- Legal Consequences: Lawsuits, regulatory fines, and potential criminal charges.
- Customer Impact: Identity theft, financial loss, and emotional distress for affected individuals.

Preventing Data Breaches

- Strong Security Measures: Implement firewalls, intrusion detection systems, and encryption.
- Employee Training: Educate employees about security best practices and social engineering tactics.
- Regular Security Audits: Identify vulnerabilities and implement corrective actions.
- Incident Response Plan: Develop a comprehensive plan to respond to data breaches effectively.
- Data Backup and Recovery: Regularly back up data and test recovery procedures.

Responding to a Data Breach

- Swift Action: Contain the breach, isolate affected systems, and notify relevant parties.
- Investigation: Determine the extent of the breach and identify compromised data.
- Notification: Inform affected individuals and regulatory authorities as required.
- Remediation: Implement measures to prevent recurrence and restore systems.
- Public Relations: Manage media and public relations to mitigate reputational damage.

By understanding the threats and implementing robust security measures, organizations can significantly reduce the risk of data breaches and protect sensitive information.

THREE
THE BUSINESS OF DATA

Data has emerged as the new oil of the digital economy. Once a mere byproduct of operations, it is now a strategic asset that drives innovation, efficiency, and competitive advantage. From the bustling e-commerce giants to the traditional brick-and-mortar businesses, organizations across industries are recognizing the immense potential locked within their data reservoirs. The ability to harness, analyze, and leverage data effectively has become a cornerstone for success in the modern business landscape.Data has transcended its role as a mere asset to become the lifeblood of modern businesses. In today's digital age, organizations across industries are amassing unprecedented volumes of information. This data, when harnessed effectively, can be transformed into invaluable insights, driving innovation, improving decision-making, and ultimately, achieving a competitive edge. The ability to collect, analyze, and leverage data has become a critical determinant of success in the global marketplace.Data has transcended its role as a mere asset to become the lifeblood of modern businesses. In today's digital age, organizations across industries are amassing unprecedented volumes of information. This data, when harnessed effectively, holds the potential to revolutionize operations, drive innovation, and unlock new revenue streams. From understanding customer behavior to optimizing supply chains, data-driven insights are reshaping the competitive landscape. Data has transcended its role as a mere asset to become the lifeblood of modern businesses. In today's digital age, organizations across industries are amassing unprecedented volumes of information. This data, when harnessed effectively, holds the potential to revolutionize operations, drive innovation, and unlock new revenue streams. From understanding customer behavior to optimizing supply chains, data-driven insights are reshaping the competitive landscape.

The ability to collect, process, analyze, and interpret data has become a core competency for businesses seeking to thrive. Organizations that excel at data management gain a significant advantage by making informed decisions, identifying new opportunities, and improving operational efficiency. However, the journey to becoming data-driven is complex. It requires robust data infrastructure, skilled analytics teams, and a culture that embraces data-informed decision-making.

As the volume and complexity of data continue to grow, organizations face challenges such as data quality, security, and privacy. Effective data governance and management are essential to ensure data integrity and compliance with regulations. Additionally, the ethical implications of data usage must be carefully considered to maintain public trust.

In conclusion, data is a strategic asset that can propel businesses to new heights. By investing in data capabilities and fostering a data-driven culture, organizations can unlock its full potential and gain a competitive edge in the digital economy.

Data monetization offers a compelling avenue for businesses to generate revenue from their data assets. By extracting value from data through various strategies such as data licensing, data products, and data-driven services, organizations can unlock new revenue streams and enhance profitability. However, data monetization requires careful consideration of data privacy, security, and ethical implications to build trust with customers and stakeholders. Data monetization is transforming data from a mere asset into a revenue-generating powerhouse. Businesses are discovering innovative ways to extract value from their data by creating new products, services, or insights. From selling anonymized customer data to creating data marketplaces, organizations are exploring diverse avenues to capitalize on their data assets. However, ethical considerations and data privacy regulations must be at the forefront to ensure responsible monetization practices.Data monetization is the process of converting data into revenue. This involves identifying valuable data assets, determining their potential market value, and developing strategies to capitalize on them. Whether it's selling data directly, licensing insights, or creating new products and services based on data-driven insights, successful data monetization requires a deep understanding of customer needs, market trends, and the competitive landscape.

DATA AS A STRATEGIC ASSEST

Data has evolved from a mere operational resource to a strategic asset capable of driving business growth and innovation.Similar to tangible assets like property or equipment, data holds intrinsic value when managed effectively. It provides invaluable insights into customer behavior, market trends, operational efficiency, and risk factors. Organizations that recognize data as a strategic asset invest in robust data infrastructure, advanced analytics capabilities, and a data-driven culture. This enables them to make informed decisions, identify new opportunities, and create competitive advantages. By treating data as a valuable resource and aligning data strategies with overall business objectives, organizations can unlock its full potential and drive sustainable growth. Data, when harnessed effectively, is no longer merely a byproduct of operations but a cornerstone of competitive advantage. It's a resource as valuable as financial capital, human talent, or physical assets.

Data is considered a strategic asset:

1. Informed Decision Making:

- Predictive Analytics: Data can forecast trends, market behaviors, and customer preferences, allowing businesses to make proactive decisions rather than reactive ones.
- Risk Mitigation: By analyzing past data, organizations can identify potential risks and develop strategies to mitigate them.
- Optimization: Data-driven insights can optimize processes, from supply chain management to marketing campaigns, leading to cost savings and efficiency gains.

Innovation Catalyst:

- New Product Development: Data can uncover unmet customer needs and identify opportunities for new product or service offerings.
- Business Model Innovation: By understanding customer behavior and market dynamics, businesses can explore new revenue streams and business models.
- Competitive Advantage: Data-driven innovation can create unique value propositions and differentiate a business from competitors.

Customer Centricity:

- Personalized Experiences: Data enables tailored marketing campaigns, product recommendations, and customer service interactions.
- Customer Lifetime Value: By understanding customer behavior and preferences, businesses can increase customer loyalty and lifetime value.
- Customer Acquisition: Data can help identify target audiences and optimize customer acquisition strategies.

Operational Efficiency:

- Process Optimization: Data can identify bottlenecks and inefficiencies in operations, leading to streamlined processes and cost reductions.
- Supply Chain Management: Data-driven insights can optimize inventory levels, improve forecasting, and enhance supply chain visibility.
- Quality Control: Data can be used to monitor product quality, identify defects, and improve manufacturing processes.

Competitive Advantage:

- Market Share: Data-driven companies often outperform competitors in terms of market share and profitability.
- First-Mover Advantage: Organizations that leverage data effectively can gain a first-mover advantage in their industry.
- Brand Reputation: A reputation for data-driven innovation can enhance brand image and customer trust.

To fully realize the potential of data as a strategic asset, organizations must:

- **Invest in data infrastructure**: This includes data collection, storage, and management systems.
- **Develop data analytics capabilities**: Build a team of data scientists and analysts to extract insights from data.
- **Foster a data-driven culture**: Encourage employees at all levels to use data to inform decision-making.
- **Prioritize data governance**: Ensure data quality, security, and compliance.

By treating data as a strategic asset and implementing these key steps, organizations can unlock its full potential and drive sustainable growth.

DATA MONETIZATION

Data monetization is the process of converting data into revenue. It involves identifying valuable data assets, determining their potential market value, and developing strategies to capitalize on them. Essentially, it's about finding ways to extract monetary value from the information an organization collects.

There are several strategies for data monetization:

- **Direct Data Sales:** Selling raw data or processed data to third parties. This could involve selling customer demographics, market research data, or financial information.
- **Data-as-a-Service (DaaS):** Offering data-driven services to customers. This might include providing analytics, insights, or predictive models based on the organization's data.
- **Data Licensing:** Granting licenses for data usage to other businesses. This often involves charging fees for access to specific datasets or data-driven applications.
- **Data Partnerships:** Collaborating with other companies to share data and create new products or services. These partnerships can lead to revenue sharing or equity arrangements.
- **Data-Driven Product Development:** Creating new products or services based on data insights. This involves leveraging data to identify market opportunities and develop innovative solutions.

Successful data monetization requires a deep understanding of the data's value, potential market demand, and legal and ethical considerations. It's also essential to protect data privacy and security to maintain customer trust. By effectively monetizing data, organizations can generate additional revenue streams, enhance their competitive position, and drive sustainable growth.

Challenges in Data Monetization

While data monetization holds immense potential, it's not without its challenges.

Here are some common hurdles:

Data Quality and Preparation: Ensuring data accuracy, completeness, and consistency is crucial for deriving meaningful insights. Low-quality data can hinder monetization efforts.

Data Privacy and Security: Protecting sensitive data is paramount. Compliance with regulations like GDPR and CCPA is essential to build trust and avoid legal repercussions.

Data Valuation: Determining the actual value of data can be complex. It requires understanding market demand, competitive landscape, and the potential impact of data on business outcomes.

Data Infrastructure: Effective data monetization requires a robust data infrastructure, including data storage, processing, and analytics capabilities.

Building Trust: Establishing trust with customers and partners is vital. Demonstrating transparency and responsible data handling is essential.

Competition: The data monetization landscape is becoming increasingly competitive. Differentiating value propositions is crucial.

Ethical Considerations: Monetizing data raises ethical concerns. Striking a balance between profit and responsible data usage is essential.

Addressing these challenges requires a strategic approach, including investing in data quality, implementing robust security measures, building strong data governance frameworks, and fostering a culture of data ethics.

DATA PRIVACY AND ETHICS

Data privacy and ethics have become paramount in today's data-driven world. As organizations increasingly collect and utilize personal information, the need to protect individuals' rights and ensure responsible data handling has grown exponentially.

Data Privacy

Data privacy refers to the protection of individual information from unauthorized access, collection, use, disclosure, copying, modification, or disposal. It encompasses the rights of individuals to control their personal data and how it is processed. Key components of data privacy include:

- Data Collection: Gathering data with transparency and explicit consent.
- Data Storage: Safeguarding data using appropriate security measures.
- Data Processing: Using data lawfully and fairly, with clear purposes.
- Data Sharing: Limiting data sharing to authorized parties and with appropriate safeguards.
- Data Subject Rights: Granting individuals the right to access, rectify, erase, and restrict the processing of their data.

Data Ethics

Data ethics focuses on the moral principles guiding data collection, analysis, and use. It involves considering the potential impact of data practices on individuals and society. Core principles of data ethics include:

- Accountability: Taking responsibility for data-related decisions and their consequences.
- Transparency: Being open about data collection, usage, and sharing practices.
- Fairness: Avoiding bias in data collection, analysis, and algorithms.
- Privacy: Respecting individuals' rights to control their personal information.
- Beneficence: Using data for the benefit of individuals and society.
- Non-maleficence: Avoiding harm to individuals or society through data practices.

The Intersection of Data Privacy and Ethics

Data privacy and ethics are closely intertwined. Privacy is a fundamental ethical consideration. Organizations must not only comply with data protection laws but also adopt ethical principles to build trust with individuals.

Key challenges at the intersection of data privacy and ethics include:

- Balancing privacy with innovation: Finding ways to utilize data for innovation while protecting individual rights.
- Consent management: Obtaining meaningful and informed consent from individuals.
- Data minimization: Collecting and retaining only necessary data.
- Algorithmic fairness: Ensuring that algorithms do not perpetuate biases or discrimination.
- Data breaches and security: Protecting data from unauthorized access and breaches.

By prioritizing data privacy and ethics, organizations can build trust, protect their reputation, and foster a responsible data-driven culture.

The technological landscape is evolving at an unprecedented pace, driven by a convergence of disruptive innovations. From artificial intelligence and blockchain to cloud computing and the Internet of Things, these core technologies are reshaping industries, creating new business models, and transforming the way we live and work. Understanding these fundamental shifts is essential for businesses and individuals seeking to navigate the complexities of the digital age. cloud computing to blockchain and the Internet of Things, these core technologies are reshaping industries, creating new business models, and transforming the way we live and work. Understanding these fundamental shifts is essential for businesses and individuals alike to navigate the complexities of the digital age and seize emerging opportunities.

Core technologies like AI, big data, cloud computing, and IoT are revolutionizing industries. Artificial intelligence is powering everything from self-driving cars to medical diagnoses, while big data analytics uncovers valuable insights from massive datasets. Cloud computing provides scalable infrastructure, and the Internet of Things connects devices, creating a network of intelligent objects. These technologies, combined with emerging trends like edge computing, blockchain, and augmented reality, are shaping our world and driving innovation across sectors. Artificial intelligence is powering everything from self-driving cars to medical diagnoses, while big data analytics uncovers valuable insights from massive datasets. Cloud computing provides scalable infrastructure, and the Internet of Things connects devices, creating a network of intelligent objects. These technologies, combined with emerging trends like edge computing, blockchain, and augmented reality, are shaping our world and driving innovation across sectors.

FOUR

ARTIFICIAL INTELLIGENCE AND MACHINE LEARNING

Artificial Intelligence (AI) and Machine Learning (ML) have emerged as the driving forces behind the digital revolution. These technologies, capable of mimicking human intelligence and learning from data, are reshaping industries, from healthcare and finance to transportation and entertainment. As AI and ML continue to advance at an exponential rate, their potential to transform our world is immense, raising both exciting opportunities and complex challenges.Artificial Intelligence (AI) and Machine Learning (ML) have emerged as the driving forces behind the digital revolution.These technologies, once confined to the realms of science fiction, are now integral to countless aspects of our lives. From powering recommendation systems to enabling self-driving cars, AI and ML are reshaping industries and redefining human potential. As these fields continue to advance at an exponential rate, their impact on society and business will only grow more profound.

DEEP LEARNING

Deep learning is a subset of machine learning that employs artificial neural networks with multiple layers to analyze complex patterns in large datasets. Inspired by the human brain's structure, these networks learn and improve over time, making them exceptionally adept at tasks that were once considered the exclusive domain of humans.

Unlike traditional machine learning algorithms, deep learning models can automatically learn features from raw data without significant human intervention. This ability to extract higher-level representations from data has led to groundbreaking advancements in various fields, including image and speech recognition, natural language processing, and autonomous systems.

Deep learning is a subset of machine learning that utilizes artificial neural networks with multiple layers to analyze complex patterns in vast datasets. It's inspired by the human brain's structure, where neurons communicate through interconnected networks.

Deep Learning Works

Neural Networks: At the core of deep learning are artificial neural networks, composed of interconnected nodes (neurons) organized in layers.

- **Input Layer:** Receives raw data (images, text, numbers).
- **Hidden Layers:** Process information through complex calculations. Multiple hidden layers allow for deep learning's ability to learn intricate patterns.
- **Output Layer:** Produces the final result, such as a classification, prediction, or decision.

Learning Process: Deep learning models learn from data through a process called backpropagation. The network adjusts its weights and biases (parameters) iteratively to minimize the difference between predicted and actual outputs.

Feature Learning: Unlike traditional machine learning, deep learning automatically learns relevant features from raw data. This eliminates the need for manual feature engineering.

Types of Deep Learning Architectures

- **Convolutional Neural Networks (CNNs):** Excel at image and video analysis. They employ convolutional layers to extract features from images.
- **Recurrent Neural Networks (RNNs):** Designed for sequential data, such as text, speech, and time series. They have connections that create loops, allowing them to process information over time.
- **Long Short-Term Memory (LSTM) networks:** A type of RNN that addresses the vanishing gradient problem, making them suitable for long-term dependencies.
- **Generative Adversarial Networks (GANs):** Compete two neural networks (generator and discriminator) to create highly realistic synthetic data.

Applications of Deep Learning

Deep learning has revolutionized various industries:

- **Image and Video Recognition:** Image classification, object detection, facial recognition, and video analysis.
- **Natural Language Processing (NLP):** Machine translation, sentiment analysis, text generation, and chatbots.
- **Speech Recognition:** Converting spoken language into text.
- **Drug Discovery:** Accelerating drug development by analyzing molecular structures and predicting drug interactions.
- **Autonomous Vehicles:** Enabling self-driving cars to perceive their environment and make decisions.

Challenges and Future Directions

Despite its successes, deep learning faces challenges such as:

- Data Hunger: Requires vast amounts of data for training.
- Computational Cost: Training deep learning models can be computationally expensive.
- Black Box Problem: Difficulty in understanding the decision-making process of complex models.

Future research focuses on developing more efficient algorithms, addressing privacy concerns, and exploring new applications like explainable AI and reinforcement learning.

REINFORCEMENT LEARINING

Reinforcement learning is a machine learning paradigm where an agent learns to make decisions by interacting with an environment. Unlike supervised learning, which provides labeled data, reinforcement learning focuses on learning through trial and error. The agent receives rewards or penalties based on its actions, and the goal is to maximize the cumulative reward over time.

Core Components of Reinforcement Learning

- Agent: The decision-maker that learns to interact with the environment.
- Environment: The world in which the agent operates.
- State: The current situation or condition of the environment.
- Action: The choices available to the agent in a given state.
- Reward: A numerical value indicating the desirability of a particular state or action.
- Policy: A strategy that maps states to actions.

The Reinforcement Learning Process

1. Initialization: The agent starts in an initial state.
2. Action Selection: The agent selects an action based on its current policy.
3. Environment Interaction: The agent takes the action, and the environment transitions to a new state.
4. Reward: The agent receives a reward based on the transition.

5. Learning: The agent updates its policy based on the received reward.
6. Repeat: The process continues iteratively until the agent learns an optimal policy.

Challenges and Applications

Reinforcement learning is a powerful technique, but it also presents challenges:

Exploration vs. Exploitation: The agent must balance exploring new actions with exploiting known good actions.

Credit Assignment: Determining which actions contributed to a reward can be complex.

Sparse Rewards: Some environments provide infrequent rewards, making learning difficult.

Despite these challenges, reinforcement learning has shown remarkable success in various domains:

- Game Playing: AlphaGo, Deep Blue, and other AI champions have been developed using reinforcement learning.
- Robotics: Training robots to perform complex tasks, such as walking, grasping, and manipulation.
- Finance: Algorithmic trading, portfolio management, and risk assessment.
- Healthcare: Drug discovery, personalized medicine, and healthcare resource optimization.

Reinforcement learning's ability to learn complex behaviors through interaction with the environment makes it a promising area of research with vast potential applications

Deep Q-Learning is a powerful combination of reinforcement learning and deep neural networks. It addresses the limitations of traditional Q-learning, which struggles with large state and action spaces. By using a deep neural network as a function approximator, Deep Q-Learning can handle complex environments effectively.

Deep Q-Learning Works

- **Q-Network:** A deep neural network approximates the Q-value function, which estimates the expected return for taking a specific action in a given state.
- **Experience Replay:** Instead of learning from the most recent experience, the agent stores experiences in a replay memory. This helps to break the correlation between consecutive experiences and improves learning efficiency.
- **Target Network:** To stabilize training, a separate target Q-network is used to compute the target values during updates. This helps to reduce oscillations in the learning process.

Challenges and Enhancements

While Deep Q-Learning has achieved remarkable success, it faces challenges:

- **Overestimation of Q-values:** The network can overestimate the value of actions, leading to suboptimal policies.
- **Exploration-exploitation dilemma:** Balancing exploration of new actions with exploitation of known good actions remains a challenge.

To address these issues, several enhancements have been proposed:

Double Deep Q-Learning: Reduces overestimation by using two Q-networks.

Dueling Deep Q-Learning: Separates the state value and action advantage, improving learning efficiency.

Prioritized Experience Replay: Prioritizes experiences based on their importance, accelerating learning.

Applications of Deep Q-Learning

Deep Q-Learning has found applications in various domains:

- Achieving superhuman performance in games like Atari and Go.
- Learning complex motor skills for robots.
- Developing self-driving car control policies.

- Personalizing recommendations based on user interactions.

Deep Q-Learning has significantly advanced the field of reinforcement learning, enabling agents to learn complex tasks in challenging environments.

GENERATIVE AI

Generative AI is a subset of artificial intelligence that focuses on creating new content, rather than simply analyzing or making predictions based on existing data. It employs sophisticated algorithms to generate text, images, music, video, and even code. Unlike traditional AI models, which are trained on vast amounts of data to recognize patterns, generative AI learns these patterns to create something entirely new.

At the heart of generative AI are complex neural networks capable of understanding and replicating the underlying structures of various forms of data. These models are trained on massive datasets, enabling them to generate highly realistic and creative outputs.

From crafting compelling stories and designing intricate artwork to composing music and developing innovative products, generative AI is rapidly expanding the boundaries of human creativity and problem-solving.

Generative AI Works

At the core of generative AI are complex neural networks, often referred to as generative models. These models are trained on massive datasets to learn the underlying structure and patterns of the data. Once trained, the model can generate new data instances that share similar characteristics with the training data.

Generative Adversarial Networks (GANs): This technique involves two neural networks, a generator, and a discriminator. The generator creates new data instances, while the discriminator tries to distinguish between real and generated data. This adversarial process leads to the generation of highly realistic outputs.

Variational Autoencoders (VAEs): These models compress data into a latent space and then reconstruct it. By sampling from the latent space, new data instances can be generated.

Transformer Models: Originally designed for natural language processing, transformers have been adapted for various generative tasks. They excel at capturing long-range dependencies in data.

Applications of Generative AI

The potential applications of generative AI are vast and continue to expand. Some notable examples include:

- **Content Creation:** Generating text, images, music, and videos for various purposes, such as marketing, entertainment, and design.
- **Drug Discovery:** Designing new molecules and predicting their properties.
- **Material Science:** Creating new materials with desired properties.
- **Art and Design:** Generating creative content, such as paintings, sculptures, and fashion designs.
- **Game Development:** Creating realistic environments, characters, and storylines.

Challenges and Considerations

While generative AI offers immense potential, it also presents challenges:

- **Ethical Concerns:** Deepfakes and misinformation are significant concerns related to generative AI.
- **Bias:** Generative models can perpetuate biases present in the training data.
- **Computational Resources:** Training large-scale generative models requires substantial computational power.
- **Intellectual Property:** Determining ownership of generated content can be complex.

Despite these challenges, generative AI is rapidly evolving, and its impact on various industries is expected to be profound. As research and development continue, we can anticipate even more groundbreaking applications and advancements in this exciting field.

Explainable AI (XAI) is a field of study focused on making the decisions of artificial intelligence models more understandable to humans. As AI models become increasingly complex, their decision-making processes often become opaque, earning them the moniker "black box." XAI aims to shed light on these black boxes, making AI models more transparent, accountable, and trustworthy.

The Need for Explainability

The demand for explainable AI arises from several factors:

- **Trust and Confidence:** Users are more likely to trust and rely on AI systems if they can understand how decisions are made.
- **Regulatory Compliance:** Many industries have regulations requiring transparency and accountability in decision-making processes.
- **Error Detection and Correction:** Understanding the reasons behind AI errors can help improve model performance.
- **Fairness and Bias Mitigation:** Explainability can help identify and address biases in AI models.

XAI Techniques

Various techniques are employed to make AI models more explainable:

Global Explainability: Provides insights into the overall behavior of the model.

- Feature importance: Identifies the most influential features in the model's decision-making.
- Partial dependence plots: Shows how model output changes with respect to a specific feature.

Local Explainability: Focuses on explaining individual predictions.

- ○ LIME (Local Interpretable Model-Agnostic Explanations): Creates a simplified model around a specific prediction to understand its contribution.
- ○ SHAP (SHapley Additive exPlanations): Assigns contributions to each feature in a prediction based on game theory.

Model-Agnostic vs. Model-Specific: Some XAI techniques work with any model type (model-agnostic), while others are tailored to specific model architectures (model-specific).

Challenges and Future Directions

While XAI has made significant progress, challenges remain:

- Trade-off between Accuracy and Explainability: Sometimes, making a model more explainable can reduce its accuracy.
- Complexity of Explanations: Explanations should be understandable to both technical and non-technical audiences.
- Causality vs. Correlation: XAI often focuses on correlations, but establishing causal relationships is more challenging.

Despite these challenges, XAI is a rapidly evolving field. Future research will likely focus on developing more sophisticated techniques, addressing the trade-off between accuracy and explainability, and ensuring that explanations are meaningful and actionable.

Local Interpretable Model-Agnostic Explanations

Let's delve deeper into LIME (Local Interpretable Model-Agnostic Explanations). It's a popular XAI technique that provides local explanations for the predictions of any machine learning model, regardless of its complexity.

LIME Works

1. **Perturbation:** LIME perturbs the original data instance by slightly modifying its features.
2. **Model Prediction:** The perturbed instances are fed into the black-box model to obtain predictions.

3. **Simple Model Training:** A simple, interpretable model (like a linear model) is trained on the perturbed instances and their corresponding predictions.
4. **Explanation Generation:** The interpretable model is used to explain the prediction of the original instance by assigning weights to the features based on their importance.

Advantages of LIME

- Model-Agnostic: Applicable to any machine learning model.
- Local Explanations: Provides insights into specific predictions, not just global behavior.
- Interpretability: The generated explanations are easy to understand.

Applications of LIME
LIME has found applications in various domains:

- **Healthcare:** Explaining the reasons behind medical diagnoses and treatment recommendations.
- **Finance:** Understanding credit risk assessments and fraud detection models.
- **Autonomous Vehicles:** Explaining the decisions made by self-driving cars.

While LIME is a powerful tool, it's essential to consider its limitations, such as the potential for instability with complex datasets and the challenge of explaining interactions between feature

FIVE

BIG DATA ANALYTICS

Big data analytics is the process of examining large volumes of data to uncover hidden patterns, correlations, market trends, and customer preferences that can help organizations make informed business decisions. In today's data-driven world, organizations are inundated with vast amounts of information from diverse sources.

Big data analytics emerges as a powerful tool for extracting valuable insights from this overwhelming volume of data. By applying advanced statistical techniques and machine learning algorithms, businesses can uncover hidden patterns, correlations, and trends that drive informed decision-making, optimize operations, and unlock new opportunities It involves collecting, cleaning, storing, processing, analyzing, and visualizing data to extract valuable insights.

The Five V's of Big Data

Big data is characterized by its volume, velocity, variety, veracity, and value:

- Volume: Massive amounts of data generated from various sources.
- Velocity: Data is generated at high speed and needs to be processed quickly.

- Variety: Data comes in different formats, structured, unstructured, and semi-structured.
- Veracity: Data quality can vary, and it's essential to ensure accuracy and reliability.
- Value: Extracting meaningful insights from data to create business value.

The Big Data Analytics Process

1. Data Collection: Gathering data from various sources like social media, sensors, and customer interactions.
2. Data Storage: Storing data in efficient and scalable systems like Hadoop Distributed File System (HDFS) or cloud-based data warehouses.
3. Data Cleaning: Processing and preparing data by handling missing values, outliers, and inconsistencies.
4. Data Analysis: Applying statistical and machine learning techniques to uncover patterns and trends.

1. Data Visualization: Presenting insights in a clear and understandable format using charts, graphs, and dashboards.

Benefits of Big Data Analytics

- Improved decision-making: Data-driven insights support better strategic planning.
- Enhanced customer experience: Understanding customer behavior for personalized offerings.
- Increased operational efficiency: Optimizing processes and reducing costs.
- New product development: Identifying market opportunities and customer needs.
- Risk management: Detecting fraud and other potential threats.

Challenges in Big Data Analytics

- Data Quality: Ensuring data accuracy and consistency.
- Data Security: Protecting sensitive data from unauthorized access.
- Data Storage and Management: Handling massive data volumes efficiently.
- Talent Shortage: Finding skilled professionals to analyze big data.

Big data analytics has the potential to transform businesses and industries. By harnessing the power of data, organizations can gain a competitive edge and drive innovation. Big data tools are the backbone of any successful big data analytics initiative. These tools enable organizations to capture, store, process, and analyze vast amounts of data efficiently. From data ingestion to visualization, a wide range of tools is available to cater to different business needs.

Core Big Data Tools

- Hadoop: An open-source framework for storing and processing large datasets across clusters of computers.
- Spark: A fast and general-purpose cluster computing framework for big data processing.
- NoSQL Databases: Designed for handling unstructured and semi-structured data, such as MongoDB, Cassandra, and HBase.
- Data Warehousing Tools: For storing and managing large volumes of data for analysis, like Teradata and Snowflake.
- Data Integration Tools: For combining data from various sources, such as Talend and Informatica.
- Business Intelligence (BI) and Data Visualization Tools: For presenting insights in a user-friendly format, like Tableau, Power BI, and Qlik.

Choosing the Right Tools

Selecting the appropriate big data tools depends on factors such as data volume, velocity, variety, and the specific business problem being addressed. A combination of tools is often used to create a robust big data analytics solution.

HADOOP AND SPARK

Hadoop is an open-source framework designed to store and process vast amounts of data across clusters of computers. It is the cornerstone of big data processing, providing a reliable and scalable platform for handling large datasets. In an era characterized by data explosion, organizations are grappling with unprecedented volumes of information. Harnessing the power of this data is crucial for gaining a competitive edge. Big data analytics emerges as a transformative force, enabling businesses to extract valuable insights, optimize operations, and drive innovation. By employing advanced technologies and statistical methods, organizations can unlock the hidden potential within their data and make data-driven decisions that propel them forward.

Core Components of Hadoop

- **Hadoop Distributed File System (HDFS):** The distributed file system that stores data across multiple nodes, providing fault tolerance and scalability.
- **MapReduce:** A programming model for processing large datasets in parallel across clusters of computers. It involves two main steps: map and reduce.
- **Yarn:** The resource manager for Hadoop, responsible for allocating resources to applications.

How Hadoop Works

Hadoop breaks down data into large blocks and distributes them across multiple nodes in a cluster. When a job is submitted, Hadoop divides the job into smaller tasks and assigns them to different nodes for parallel processing. The results from these tasks are then combined to produce the final output.

Advantages of Hadoop

- Scalability: Handles massive datasets by adding more nodes to the cluster.

- Fault Tolerance: Data is replicated across multiple nodes for redundancy.
- Cost-Effective: Leverages commodity hardware for storage and processing.
- Flexibility: Supports various data formats and processing frameworks.

Apache Spark: The Fast and Furious

Apache Spark is a fast and general-purpose cluster computing framework designed for big data processing. It builds upon the distributed architecture of Hadoop but offers significantly faster performance and supports a wider range of workloads.

Key Features of Spark

- **In-Memory Processing:** Spark stores data in memory, leading to much faster processing speeds compared to Hadoop's disk-based approach.
- **Fault Tolerance:** Similar to Hadoop, Spark provides fault tolerance through data replication.
- **Versatility:** Supports batch processing, stream processing, SQL queries, machine learning, and graph processing.
- **Ease of Use:** Provides high-level APIs in Python, Scala, and Java, making it accessible to developers.

Spark vs Hadoop

While both Hadoop and Spark are essential tools for big data processing, they have distinct strengths:

- Hadoop is better suited for batch processing and handling massive datasets with low latency requirements.
- Spark excels in real-time processing, iterative algorithms, and machine learning workloads.

In many cases, Hadoop and Spark are used together, with Hadoop providing the underlying storage layer and Spark handling the data processing and analysis.

Challenges in Hadoop and Spark

While Hadoop and Spark are powerful tools for big data processing, they come with their own set of challenges.

Hadoop Challenges

- Complexity: Hadoop's architecture can be complex to set up and manage.
- Performance: Batch processing nature can be slow for real-time applications.
- Talent Shortage: Finding skilled Hadoop developers can be challenging.

Spark Challenges

- Resource Intensive: Spark's in-memory processing requires significant computational resources.
- Data Skew: Uneven data distribution can impact performance.
- Job Management: Managing complex Spark workflows can be intricate.

Overcoming Challenges

- **Hybrid Approaches:** Combining Hadoop and Spark can mitigate their individual drawbacks.
- **Optimization Techniques:** Techniques like data partitioning, compression, and indexing can improve performance.
- **Talent Development:** Investing in training and development programs for big data professionals.
- **Cloud-Based Solutions:** Leveraging cloud platforms can simplify management and scalability.

By understanding and addressing these challenges, organizations can effectively harness the power of Hadoop and Spark for their big data initiatives

CLOUD -BASES ANALYTICS

Cloud-based analytics is the application of analytic algorithms in the cloud to extract valuable insights from data. By leveraging the power of cloud computing, organizations can process vast amounts of data rapidly and efficiently, without the need for on-premises infrastructure. This transformative approach empowers businesses to make data-driven decisions faster, with greater agility, and at a lower cost.

Cloud-based analytics has revolutionized how organizations approach data analysis, offering scalability, flexibility, and cost-effectiveness.

Cloud-based analytics is the application of analytic algorithms in the cloud to extract valuable insights from data. By leveraging the power of cloud computing, organizations can process vast amounts of data rapidly and efficiently, without the need for on-premises infrastructure. This transformative approach empowers businesses to make data-driven decisions faster, with greater agility, and at a lower cost.

Core Components of Cloud-Based Analytics

- **Data Storage:** Cloud-based data warehouses and data lakes provide scalable and cost-effective storage for massive datasets.
- **Data Processing:** Cloud platforms offer powerful computing resources for processing and analyzing data, including tools for ETL (Extract, Transform, Load), data cleansing, and preparation.
- **Analytics Services:** Cloud providers offer a range of analytics services, such as SQL and NoSQL databases, machine learning, and data visualization.
- **Data Governance and Security:** Robust security measures and data governance frameworks are essential for protecting sensitive information.

Benefits of Cloud-Based Analytics

- Scalability: Easily adjust resources to handle varying data volumes and processing needs.
- Cost-Efficiency: Pay-as-you-go pricing models eliminate upfront infrastructure investments.
- Speed and Performance: Leverage high-performance cloud computing resources for faster insights.
- Accessibility: Access data and analytics tools from anywhere with an internet connection.
- Innovation: Explore advanced analytics capabilities like machine learning and AI.

Cloud-Based Analytics Use Cases

- Customer Analytics: Gain deeper insights into customer behavior, preferences, and churn.
- Financial Analytics: Detect fraud, optimize risk management, and improve investment decisions.
- Marketing Analytics: Measure campaign performance, personalize marketing efforts, and identify new customer segments.
- Supply Chain Optimization: Improve inventory management, logistics, and supply chain visibility.
- Healthcare Analytics: Analyze patient data to improve outcomes and reduce costs.

Challenges and Considerations

- Data Security and Privacy: Protecting sensitive data in the cloud is paramount.
- Data Governance: Establishing data ownership, quality, and usage policies.
- Vendor Lock-In: Dependence on cloud providers can create challenges when switching platforms.
- Network Latency: High latency can impact real-time analytics performance.

Cloud-based analytics is rapidly transforming how businesses operate. By harnessing the power of the cloud, organizations can unlock the full potential of their data and gain a competitive advantage. Cloud data warehouses are cloud-based repositories for storing, retrieving, and manipulating large datasets to support analytics projects.

They offer scalability, agility, and cost savings compared to traditional on-premises data warehouses.

Key Features of Cloud Data Warehouses

- Scalability: Easily adjust storage and processing capacity to meet changing data volumes.
- Performance: Leverage powerful cloud infrastructure for rapid query execution.
- Cost-Efficiency: Pay-as-you-go pricing models eliminate upfront investments.
- Data Integration: Seamlessly integrate data from various sources, including on-premises systems.
- Data Governance: Built-in security and compliance features to protect sensitive data.

Benefits of Cloud Data Warehouses

- Accelerated Time-to-Market: Quickly deploy and scale data warehouses to support new business initiatives.
- Improved Decision Making: Access real-time insights to make informed business decisions.
- Enhanced Customer Experience: Deliver personalized experiences based on customer data.
- Cost Reduction: Lower IT infrastructure costs and operational expenses.

Cloud Data Warehouse Providers

Major cloud providers offer their own cloud data warehouse solutions:

- Amazon Redshift: A fully managed, petabyte-scale data warehouse service.
- Google BigQuery: A serverless, highly scalable data warehouse for analytics.
- Snowflake: A cloud-native data platform that offers flexibility and performance.
- Microsoft Azure Synapse Analytics: A unified analytics service combining data warehousing and big data processing.

By leveraging cloud data warehouses, organizations can build a solid foundation for their data analytics initiatives and derive maximum value from their data assets.

Data visualization and storytelling are powerful tools for transforming raw data into compelling narratives that drive understanding and action. By combining the art of visual communication with the science of data analysis, organizations can effectively communicate complex information to diverse audiences. Data visualization translates data into visual representations like charts, graphs, and maps, making patterns and trends easily understandable. When coupled with storytelling, data becomes a powerful tool for engaging audiences and driving decision-making.

Effective data visualization and storytelling go beyond mere aesthetics. They require a deep understanding of the data, the target audience, and the desired outcome. By crafting a compelling narrative around the data, organizations can inspire action, influence opinions, and uncover new insights.

Data visualization and storytelling are powerful tools for transforming raw data into compelling narratives that drive understanding and action. By combining the art of visual communication with the science of data analysis, organizations can effectively communicate complex information to diverse audiences. Data visualization translates data into visual representations like charts, graphs, and maps, making patterns and trends easily understandable. When coupled with storytelling, data becomes a powerful tool for engaging audiences and driving decision-making.

The Art of Data Visualization

Data visualization is the process of representing information graphically. It involves selecting appropriate chart types, designing effective layouts, and choosing colors and fonts that enhance readability. Effective visualizations:

- Simplify complexity: Break down complex data into easily digestible formats.
- Reveal patterns: Highlight trends, correlations, and outliers.
- Facilitate understanding: Make information accessible to a wide audience.
- Inspire action: Encourage data-driven decision-making.

Common visualization types include:

- Bar charts: Comparing categorical data.
- Line charts: Showing trends over time.
- Scatter plots: Identifying relationships between numerical variables.
- Histograms: Displaying data distribution.
- Maps: Visualizing geographic data.
- Infographics: Combining visuals and text for storytelling.

The Science of Data Storytelling

Data storytelling goes beyond creating visually appealing charts. It involves crafting a narrative around the data that resonates with the audience. Effective data storytelling:

- Defines a clear purpose: Identifies the key message or insight to be conveyed.
- Understands the audience: Tailors the story to the target audience's knowledge and interests.
- Structures the narrative: Creates a logical flow of information with a beginning, middle, and end.

- Uses visuals effectively: Selects and combines visualizations to support the story.
- Engages the audience: Uses storytelling techniques like metaphors, analogies, and emotions.

By combining data visualization and storytelling, organizations can create impactful data narratives that drive business results.

While data visualization is essential, crafting a compelling narrative around the data is equally crucial. Effective data storytelling involves several challenges and best practices:

Challenges in Data Storytelling

- Identifying the Right Story: Extracting a compelling narrative from complex data can be challenging.
- Audience Understanding: Tailoring the story to different audiences with varying levels of data literacy.
- Visual Overload: Avoiding overwhelming the audience with too much information.
- Ethical Considerations: Ensuring data is presented accurately and without bias.

Best Practices in Data Storytelling

- Understand their level of data literacy, interests, and expectations.
- Develop a clear and engaging story before creating visualizations.
- Select visualizations that effectively communicate the story.
- Maintain a cohesive visual identity throughout the presentation.
- Use storytelling techniques like characters, conflict, and resolution.
- Refine the story based on feedback and testing.

Advanced Data Visualization Techniques

Beyond basic charts and graphs, advanced visualization techniques can provide deeper insights:

- **Interactive Visualizations:** Allow users to explore data dynamically.
- **Geovisualizations:** Map data to geographic locations for spatial analysis.
- **Network Diagrams:** Visualize relationships between entities.
- **Sankey Diagrams:** Show flows and quantities between different stages.
- **Treemaps:** Display hierarchical data using nested rectangles.

By mastering these techniques and following best practices, you can create data stories that inform, inspire, and drive action.

INTERACTIVE DASHBOARD

Interactive dashboards are dynamic visual representations of data that allow users to explore, analyze, and interact with information in real-time. Unlike static reports, interactive dashboards empower users to drill down into details, filter data, and uncover insights at their fingertips.

Key Components of Interactive Dashboards

Data Connectivity: Integration with various data sources, including databases, spreadsheets, and cloud applications.

Data Visualization: Effective use of charts, graphs, and maps to represent data clearly and concisely.

Interactivity: Features like filtering, drilling down, zooming, and highlighting to explore data dynamically.

Customization: Ability to personalize dashboard layouts and content to meet individual needs.

Real-time Updates: Displaying up-to-date information to support timely decision-making.

Benefits of Interactive Dashboards

- Improved Decision Making: By providing timely and actionable insights, dashboards support data-driven decisions.

- Enhanced Collaboration: Enable teams to work together by sharing dashboards and insights.
- Increased Efficiency: Streamline data analysis and reporting processes.
- Better Storytelling: Effectively communicate complex data narratives through visualizations.
- Empowerment: Give users control over data exploration and discovery.

Common Use Cases for Interactive Dashboards

- Sales: Track sales performance, customer acquisition, and sales pipeline.
- Marketing: Analyze campaign effectiveness, customer segmentation, and ROI.
- Finance: Monitor financial performance, track key metrics, and identify trends.
- Operations: Optimize processes, monitor KPIs, and identify bottlenecks.
- Human Resources: Analyze employee performance, track workforce demographics, and measure training effectiveness.

Best Practices for Creating Effective Dashboards

- Focus on Key Metrics: Prioritize the most important indicators.
- Clear and Concise Visualizations: Use charts and graphs that are easy to understand.
- Interactive Elements: Incorporate filters, drill-downs, and other interactive features.
- User-Centric Design: Consider the needs and preferences of the end-users.
- Regular Updates: Ensure data is refreshed frequently to provide accurate insights.

By effectively leveraging interactive dashboards, organizations can unlock the full potential of their data and gain a competitive advantage.

The information you've provided is a great summary of interactive dashboards! Here's what we can do next:

Dive into Specific Areas: You've identified key components, benefits, use cases, and best practices. Would you like to explore any of these areas in more detail. For example, we could delve into specific data visualization techniques for dashboards or discuss advanced interaction features.

Examples and Case Studies: Seeing real-world examples can be very helpful. Would you like to explore some successful implementations of interactive dashboards in different industries (e.g., sales dashboard, marketing dashboard)

Creating Interactive Dashboards: If you're interested in building your own interactive dashboards, I can provide resources on popular tools and platforms like Tableau, Power BI, and Google Data Studio.

Comparison with Static Reports: We could discuss the advantages and disadvantages of interactive dashboards compared to traditional static reports.

AUGMENTED ANALYTICS

Augmented analytics is a class of analytics powered by artificial intelligence (AI) and machine learning (ML) that expands a human's ability to interact with data at a contextual

level. It involves the integration of AI and ML techniques into data analytics tools to automate and enhance the analysis process, making it accessible to a broader range of users.

Augmented Analytics Works

Augmented analytics leverages AI and ML to:

- **Automate data preparation:** Cleaning, transforming, and preparing data for analysis.
- **Generate insights:** Identifying patterns, trends, and anomalies in data automatically.

- **Create visualizations**: Generating appropriate visualizations to represent insights effectively.
- **Provide explanations**: Offering clear and concise explanations for insights and recommendations.
- **Enable natural language interaction**: Allowing users to interact with data using everyday language.

Benefits of Augmented Analytics

- Democratization of data: Makes analytics accessible to a wider audience, not just data scientists.
- Faster time to insights: Automates routine tasks, allowing users to focus on higher-level analysis.
- Improved decision making: Provides deeper insights and recommendations to support better decisions.
- Enhanced productivity: Streamlines the analytics process, increasing efficiency.
- Augmented creativity: Helps analysts explore new data perspectives and uncover hidden patterns.

Key Components of Augmented Analytics

- Enables users to interact with data using natural language queries.
- Automates data preparation, feature engineering, and model building.
- Creates interactive and informative visualizations.
- Provides recommendations and insights based on data analysis.

Challenges and Considerations

- Data Quality: The quality of the underlying data directly impacts the accuracy of augmented analytics insights.
- Explainability: Ensuring that AI-generated insights are understandable and trustworthy is crucial.

- Bias: Addressing potential biases in data and algorithms is essential.
- User Adoption: Overcoming resistance to change and educating users about augmented analytics.

Augmented analytics is transforming the way organizations leverage data. By automating routine tasks and providing deeper insights, it empowers a wider range of users to make data-driven decisions and drive business growth.

Challenges in Implementing Augmented Analytics

While augmented analytics holds immense promise, its implementation comes with several challenges:

- The accuracy and completeness of data are crucial for generating reliable insights. Poor data quality can lead to inaccurate recommendations and hinder the effectiveness of augmented analytics.
- Understanding how AI algorithms arrive at their conclusions is essential for trust and adoption. Black-box models can pose challenges in this regard.
- Unconscious biases can be embedded in data and algorithms, leading to unfair or discriminatory outcomes.
- Overcoming resistance to change and fostering a data-driven culture is crucial for successful implementation.
- Protecting sensitive data while leveraging AI and ML requires robust security measures.
- Organizations may face a shortage of skilled professionals with expertise in augmented analytics.

Addressing these challenges is essential for realizing the full potential of augmented analytics.

DATA JOURNALISM

Data journalism is a form of journalism that involves the systematic gathering, analysis, and presentation of data to inform and engage the public. It blends traditional journalism with data analysis, statistics, and visualization to uncover hidden stories within vast datasets.

Core Principles of Data Journalism

Data-Driven Storytelling: Journalists use data as the foundation for their narratives, revealing trends, patterns, and anomalies.

Transparency and Accountability: Data journalists prioritize transparency by sharing their methodologies and data sources.

Public Interest: Stories are focused on issues that matter to the public, often involving social, economic, or political matters.

Innovation: Data journalists experiment with new tools and techniques to enhance storytelling.

The Data Journalism Process

1. **Data Acquisition:** Gathering relevant data from various sources, including government databases, surveys, and social media.
2. **Data Cleaning and Preparation:** Ensuring data accuracy, consistency, and completeness.
3. **Data Analysis:** Exploring data to identify patterns, trends, and anomalies.
4. **Data Visualization:** Creating compelling visuals to communicate findings effectively.
5. **Storytelling:** Weaving data into a narrative that is engaging and informative.

Impact of Data Journalism

Data journalism has transformed the way news is produced and consumed. It has led to groundbreaking investigations, exposed systemic issues, and empowered citizens. By providing data-driven insights into complex problems, data journalism contributes to a more informed and engaged public.

THE INTERNET OF THINGS(IOT) AND DATA SCIENCE

The Internet of Things (IoT) and data science represent a powerful synergy that is transforming industries and redefining how we interact with the world. IoT devices generate massive volumes of data at unprecedented speeds, creating a data-rich environment ripe for exploration. Data science provides the tools and techniques to extract meaningful insights from this data deluge, enabling organizations to make informed decisions, optimize operations, and create innovative solutions.The Internet of Things (IoT) and data science are converging to reshape industries and redefine our daily lives. IoT devices, ranging from wearables to industrial sensors, generate vast amounts of data at an unprecedented rate. Data science, with its focus on extracting insights from complex datasets, has become indispensable in unlocking the full potential of this data. Together, IoT and data science form a powerful synergy, driving innovation and creating new opportunities across various sectors.

The Internet of Things (IoT) and data science are two technological forces converging to reshape industries and redefine our daily lives. IoT, a network of interconnected devices capable of collecting and exchanging data, generates vast amounts of information at an unprecedented rate. Data science, the field of extracting insights from data, is essential for unlocking the true potential of this data deluge.

The Intersection of IoT and Data Science

The synergy between IoT and data science is creating a new era of possibilities. IoT devices act as data generators, continuously feeding information into the data science pipeline. This data, once processed and analyzed, provides valuable insights that can be used to optimize processes, improve decision-making, and create new business models.

Key areas where IoT and data science intersect:

- **Data Collection and Management:** IoT devices generate massive amounts of data that need to be efficiently collected, stored, and processed.
- **Data Preprocessing:** Cleaning and preparing IoT data for analysis is crucial to ensure accurate insights.
- **Data Analysis and Modeling:** Applying statistical and machine learning techniques to uncover patterns and trends in IoT data.

- **Predictive Analytics:** Using historical data to forecast future outcomes and optimize operations.
- **Prescriptive Analytics:** Recommending actions based on data-driven insights.

Challenges and Opportunities

While the combination of IoT and data science offers immense potential, it also presents challenges:

- Data Volume and Velocity: IoT devices generate vast amounts of data at high speed, requiring efficient data management and processing.
- Data Quality: Ensuring data accuracy and reliability is crucial for deriving meaningful insights.
- Data Security: Protecting sensitive data generated by IoT devices is paramount.
- Skill Gap: Finding skilled data scientists with expertise in IoT is a challenge.

Despite these challenges, the combination of IoT and data science is driving innovation across industries, from smart cities and healthcare to manufacturing and agriculture. As technology continues to advance, we can expect even more groundbreaking applications and breakthroughs in this field.

Use Cases of IoT and Data Science

The combination of IoT and data science has led to transformative applications across various industries. Let's explore some key use cases:

Smart Cities

- **Traffic Management:** IoT sensors collect real-time traffic data, which is analyzed to optimize traffic flow, reduce congestion, and improve public transportation.
- **Smart Grids:** IoT devices monitor energy consumption, enabling utilities to optimize grid operations, detect anomalies, and

implement demand-response programs.

- **Waste Management:** IoT sensors in waste bins track fill levels, optimizing waste collection routes and reducing costs.

Healthcare

- **Remote Patient Monitoring:** Wearable devices and sensors collect patient data, enabling remote monitoring and early detection of health issues.
- **Predictive Maintenance:** IoT sensors monitor medical equipment, predicting failures and preventing downtime.
- **Drug Discovery:** Analyzing IoT data from patient sensors can accelerate drug development and personalized medicine.

Manufacturing

- **Predictive Maintenance:** IoT sensors monitor equipment health, allowing for predictive maintenance and reducing downtime.
- **Supply Chain Optimization:** IoT devices track product movement, enabling real-time visibility and optimizing logistics.
- **Quality Control:** IoT sensors monitor production processes, ensuring product quality and identifying defects.

Agriculture

- **Precision Agriculture:** IoT sensors collect data on soil conditions, weather, and crop health, optimizing resource utilization and maximizing yield.
- **Livestock Monitoring:** IoT devices track animal health, behavior, and location, improving livestock management.
- **Supply Chain Optimization:** IoT sensors monitor food product conditions, ensuring food safety and reducing waste.

Challenges and Opportunities

While the potential of IoT and data science is vast, several challenges persist:

- Protecting sensitive data generated by IoT devices is crucial.
- Ensuring seamless communication between different IoT devices and platforms.
- Handling the massive volume of data generated by IoT devices.
- Finding skilled professionals with expertise in IoT and data science.

Despite these challenges, the combination of IoT and data science offers unprecedented opportunities for innovation and growth. As technology continues to advance, we can expect to see even more groundbreaking applications emerging in the years to come.

IOT DATA CHALLENGES

IoT devices generate vast amounts of data at unprecedented speeds, presenting unique challenges for data management and analysis. Key challenges include:

- The sheer volume of data generated by IoT devices can overwhelm traditional data management systems. Real-time processing capabilities are essential to handle the high velocity of data.
- IoT data comes in various formats, structured, unstructured, and semi-structured, making it complex to integrate and analyze.
- Ensuring data accuracy, completeness, and consistency is crucial for deriving meaningful insights. Noise and errors in IoT data can impact analysis results.
- Protecting sensitive data collected by IoT devices is paramount. Data breaches and privacy violations can have severe consequences.
- Storing and processing massive amounts of IoT data can be expensive.

- Deriving actionable insights from IoT data requires real-time processing capabilities.
- Integrating IoT data with existing enterprise systems and applications can be complex.

Overcoming these challenges is essential for unlocking the full potential of IoT data.

EDGE COMPUTING

Edge computing is a distributed computing paradigm that brings computation and data storage closer to the sources of data.

Instead of relying solely on centralized data centers, edge computing pushes processing power and storage to the network's edge, where data is generated.

Edge Computing Work

Imagine trying to access a file stored on a distant server. It takes time for the request to travel, the server to process it, and the data to return. This delay, known as latency, can be frustrating. Edge computing solves this by placing computing resources closer to the user.

For example, a video streaming service might use edge servers to store popular content in different geographical locations. When you request a video, the nearest edge server delivers it, reducing buffering time significantly.

Benefits of Edge Computing

- **Reduced Latency:** By processing data closer to its source, edge computing dramatically reduces response times. This is crucial for applications like real-time gaming, augmented reality, and autonomous vehicles.
- **Improved Performance:** Edge computing can handle increased data volumes and processing demands more efficiently than centralized data centers.
- **Enhanced Reliability:** With data processed locally, applications are less susceptible to network outages or disruptions.

- **Data Privacy:** Edge computing can help protect sensitive data by processing it closer to its origin, reducing the risk of data breaches.
- **Cost Reduction:** By offloading processing tasks from centralized data centers, organizations can potentially lower operational costs.

Use Cases of Edge Computing

- **IoT (Internet of Things):** Edge computing is essential for processing vast amounts of data generated by IoT devices in real-time. Applications include smart cities, industrial automation, and agriculture.
- **Autonomous Vehicles:** Edge computing enables self-driving cars to make split-second decisions based on data from sensors and cameras.
- **Augmented and Virtual Reality:** Low latency is crucial for immersive experiences. Edge computing ensures smooth interactions and reduces motion sickness.
- **Video Streaming:** By delivering content closer to users, edge computing improves video quality and reduces buffering.
- **Retail:** Edge computing can enable real-time inventory management, personalized recommendations, and improved customer experiences.

Challenges and Future of Edge Computing

While edge computing offers significant advantages, it also presents challenges such as security, management, and cost. However, as technology continues to advance, these challenges are being addressed.

The future of edge computing is bright, with potential applications expanding into various industries. As 5G and other advanced networks become more widespread, edge computing is poised to become a critical component of our digital infrastructure

Use Case: Autonomous Vehicles

A fascinating application of edge computing is in the realm of autonomous vehicles. These self-driving cars generate massive amounts of data from sensors, cameras, and other devices. To make real-time decisions, such as avoiding obstacles or responding to traffic changes, this data needs to be processed instantaneously.

Edge computing enables vehicles to process critical data locally, reducing latency and ensuring quick responses. For instance, a car equipped with edge computing can analyze sensor data to detect a pedestrian crossing without relying on cloud-based processing.

Benefits:

Faster decision-making reduces the risk of accidents.

Real-time data processing optimizes vehicle performance.

Edge computing allows vehicles to operate even in areas with poor network coverage.

The Technology Behind Edge Computing

While the concept of edge computing might seem straightforward, the underlying technology is complex. Key components include:

- These are physical devices located at the network's edge, such as IoT sensors, smartphones, or servers.
- These are more powerful computing devices deployed closer to the data source, capable of handling complex computations.
- A robust network is essential to connect edge devices and servers with the core cloud.
- Software platforms that manage and orchestrate edge resources.

PREDICTIVE MAINTENANCE

Predictive maintenance is a data-driven approach to equipment maintenance that aims to predict when a piece of equipment is likely to fail. By analyzing real-time data from sensors and historical maintenance records, organizations can schedule maintenance proactively, preventing costly breakdowns and maximizing equipment lifespan.

Predictive Maintenance Work

1. **Data Collection:** Sensors are installed on equipment to gather data on various parameters such as temperature, vibration, pressure, and performance metrics.
2. **Data Analysis:** The collected data is processed using advanced analytics and machine learning algorithms to identify patterns and anomalies that indicate potential equipment failures.
3. **Predictive Modeling:** Based on the analysis, predictive models are created to forecast when equipment is likely to fail.
4. **Maintenance Scheduling:** Maintenance tasks are scheduled proactively based on the predictions, ensuring that equipment is serviced before it breaks down.

Benefits of Predictive Maintenance

- By preventing unplanned breakdowns, predictive maintenance significantly improves equipment availability.
- By optimizing maintenance schedules, organizations can avoid unnecessary maintenance tasks, leading to cost savings.
- Early detection of equipment failures can help prevent accidents and injuries.
- Predictive maintenance helps optimize asset utilization and production processes.
- addressing issues before they escalate, the overall lifespan of equipment can be extended.

Use Cases of Predictive Maintenance

Predictive maintenance can be applied across various industries, including:

- **Manufacturing:** Monitoring equipment health to prevent production line disruptions.
- **Aviation:** Predicting engine failures to ensure flight safety.
- **Energy:** Optimizing maintenance schedules for power plants and wind turbines.

- **Oil and Gas:** Preventing equipment failures in remote and hazardous environments.
- **Transportation:** Predicting vehicle breakdowns to improve fleet management.

Challenges and Considerations

While predictive maintenance offers significant benefits, it also presents challenges:

- Accurate and reliable data is essential for effective predictive modeling.
- Implementing a comprehensive sensor network can be expensive.
- Skilled data scientists are needed to develop and maintain predictive models.
- Adopting a predictive maintenance culture requires changes in processes and mindsets.

Despite these challenges, the potential benefits of predictive maintenance make it a valuable investment for many organizations. As technology continues to advance, we can expect to see even more sophisticated predictive maintenance solutions emerge.

Industry Focus: Aviation

The aviation industry is a prime example of where predictive maintenance is critical. The safety and reliability of aircraft are paramount, and even minor equipment failures can have catastrophic consequences.

Engine Health Monitoring: By continuously monitoring engine parameters like temperature, vibration, and oil pressure, airlines can predict engine failures before they occur. This helps in scheduling maintenance proactively, preventing unexpected engine failures during flight.

Component Wear and Tear: Predictive maintenance can track the wear and tear of components like landing gear, brakes, and avionics. By identifying potential issues early on, airlines can replace components before they fail, reducing downtime and increasing aircraft availability.

Cost Savings: Proactive maintenance reduces the risk of costly emergency repairs and unscheduled aircraft groundings.

Technology Spotlight: Machine Learning

Machine learning is the backbone of predictive maintenance. It enables the analysis of vast amounts of data to identify patterns and anomalies that indicate potential equipment failures.

Algorithm Selection: Choosing the right machine learning algorithm is crucial. Techniques like time series analysis, regression, and classification are commonly used for predictive maintenance.

Feature Engineering: Extracting relevant features from raw data is essential for building accurate predictive models. This involves transforming data into a format that can be easily understood by machine learning algorithms.

Model Evaluation: Continuously evaluating the performance of predictive models is vital to ensure their accuracy and reliability. Techniques like cross-validation and A/B testing can be used for this purpose.

SIX

INDUSTRY APPLICATION

Industry refers to the collective group of organizations involved in producing or handling a specific type of product or service. It encompasses the transformation of raw materials into finished goods, as well as the provision of services that cater to various needs. Industries are the backbone of economies, driving economic growth, generating employment, and fostering innovation. From manufacturing and agriculture to technology and finance, industries play a crucial role in shaping societies and improving living standards.

Third-party industry applications are specialized software solutions designed to address specific needs within particular industries. These applications are developed and maintained by external companies, distinct from the core business operations of the organizations that utilize them. By leveraging the expertise of specialized developers, businesses can access cutting-edge technology and industry-specific functionalities without the burden of in-house development. This allows companies to focus on their core competencies while benefiting from the efficiency and innovation offered by these applications. Tailored to meet the unique requirements of a particular industry, such as healthcare, finance, or retail. Created and maintained by independent software vendors (ISVs). Designed to seamlessly integrate with existing systems and workflows. Able to adapt to changing business needs and growth. Regularly updated with new features and enhancements. The adoption of third-party industry applications has become increasingly prevalent due to the rapid pace of technological advancements and the growing complexity of business operations. These applications offer a wide range of benefits, including increased productivity, improved decision-making, enhanced customer experience, and cost reduction.

DATA SCIENCE IN HEALTHCARE

Data science is revolutionizing the healthcare industry by unlocking the immense potential hidden within vast amounts of patient data. By employing advanced analytical techniques, machine learning algorithms, and statistical models, healthcare providers can extract valuable insights to improve patient outcomes, optimize operations, and accelerate medical research. This transformative field is enabling precision medicine, early disease detection, efficient drug discovery, and streamlined healthcare delivery. For instance, data science can be used to identify high-risk patients, predict disease outbreaks, optimize treatment plans, and develop new therapies. The integration of data-driven insights into healthcare is poised to enhance patient care, reduce costs, and drive innovation.

PRECISION MEDICINE

Precision medicine is a revolutionary approach to healthcare that focuses on tailoring medical treatments and prevention strategies to individual patients based on their unique genetic makeup, environment, and lifestyle. By analyzing a patient's specific biological and clinical information, healthcare providers can predict more accurately which treatments will be most effective and which ones to avoid. This paradigm shift from a "one-size-fits-all" approach to a personalized one holds immense promise for improving patient outcomes. By identifying the underlying causes of disease at a molecular level, precision medicine aims to prevent, diagnose, and treat diseases more effectively. This includes developing targeted therapies, minimizing side effects, and optimizing treatment plans.

Ultimately, precision medicine has the potential to transform healthcare by enhancing patient care, reducing healthcare costs, and accelerating drug discovery.

Precision medicine, also known as personalized medicine, is a revolutionary approach to healthcare that aims to optimize prevention and treatment strategies for individual patients based on their unique biological, environmental, and lifestyle factors. By leveraging advancements in genomics, molecular biology, and data analytics, healthcare providers can gain a deeper understanding of a patient's disease and develop tailored interventions.

Key components of precision medicine:

Genomics: Analyzing an individual's genetic makeup to identify genetic variations associated with disease risk, progression, and treatment response.

Molecular profiling: Studying the molecular characteristics of a disease, including proteins, RNA, and metabolites, to identify specific targets for therapy.

Clinical data: Integrating electronic health records, medical imaging, and other clinical data to create a comprehensive patient profile.

Lifestyle and environmental factors: Considering the impact of a patient's lifestyle, diet, and environmental exposures on their health.

Applications of precision medicine:

- **Cancer treatment:** Identifying specific genetic mutations in tumor cells to select targeted therapies, improving treatment efficacy and reducing side effects.
- **Rare diseases:** Diagnosing and treating rare diseases more effectively by identifying underlying genetic causes.
- **Drug development:** Accelerating drug discovery by focusing on specific patient populations, increasing the likelihood of successful clinical trials.

- **Preventive medicine:** Predicting disease risk based on genetic and lifestyle factors, enabling personalized prevention strategies.

Challenges and considerations:

- Data privacy and security: Protecting sensitive patient information is crucial.
- Ethical implications: Addressing issues related to genetic discrimination and informed consent.
- Cost: Implementing precision medicine can be expensive due to the need for advanced technologies and specialized expertise.
- Infrastructure: Building the necessary infrastructure to collect, analyze, and interpret vast amounts of data is challenging.

Despite these challenges, precision medicine holds immense potential to transform healthcare by improving patient outcomes, reducing healthcare costs, and accelerating medical research. As technology continues to advance and our understanding of human biology deepens, precision medicine is poised to become the standard of care.

Oncology

Cancer treatment has been significantly transformed by precision medicine. By analyzing a tumor's genetic makeup, doctors can identify specific molecular targets and prescribe targeted therapies.

- **Tumor profiling:** Advanced techniques like genomic sequencing allow for detailed analysis of tumor cells, revealing specific genetic mutations.
- **Targeted therapies:** Drugs designed to attack these specific mutations can be administered, often with fewer side effects than traditional chemotherapy.
- **Immunotherapy:** Precision medicine has also enhanced immunotherapy treatments by identifying patients most likely

to respond to these therapies based on their tumor's immune profile.

For example, patients with lung cancer harboring the EGFR mutation can benefit greatly from EGFR inhibitors, which target this specific genetic alteration.

Rare Diseases

Precision medicine has been a game-changer for patients with rare diseases, often characterized by a lack of effective treatments.

- **Genetic diagnosis:** By analyzing a patient's genetic code, rare diseases can be diagnosed more accurately and efficiently.
- **Patient communities:** Connecting patients with similar rare diseases through patient registries facilitates data sharing and research collaboration.
- **Drug development:** Identifying the underlying genetic causes of rare diseases can accelerate the development of targeted therapies.

For instance, patients with cystic fibrosis, a rare genetic disorder, can now benefit from targeted therapies that address the underlying genetic defect, improving lung function and quality of life. These are just a few examples of how precision medicine is revolutionizing healthcare. As technology continues to advance, we can expect to see even more groundbreaking applications in the years to come.

DRUG DISCOVERY

Drug discovery is a complex and time-consuming process that involves the identification, development, and testing of new medications.

It's a critical step in the healthcare industry, as it leads to the development of treatments for various diseases and conditions.

The journey typically begins with target identification. Scientists pinpoint specific molecules or proteins involved in a disease process. Once a target is identified, researchers develop compounds that can interact with this target and potentially modify its function. This process often involves high-throughput screening to test thousands of compounds rapidly. Medicinal chemistry plays a crucial role in optimizing these compounds to improve their efficacy, safety, and drug-like properties. Computational methods, such as molecular modeling and virtual screening, are increasingly used to accelerate the drug discovery process. Once promising compounds are identified, they undergo rigorous testing, including preclinical studies in animals to assess safety and efficacy. Successful compounds then advance to clinical trials involving human subjects to evaluate their safety and effectiveness in treating the target disease. The entire drug discovery and development process can take several years and billions of dollars, with high rates of failure. However, when successful, it leads to life-saving medications that improve the quality of life for countless patients.

The Drug Discovery Process

Drug discovery is a complex and iterative process that involves multiple stages, each with its own challenges and complexities.

Target Identification and Validation

The initial step is to identify a specific molecule or protein (the target) involved in a disease process. This requires a deep understanding of the disease's biology and pathology. Once a target is identified, it must be validated to ensure that inhibiting or activating it will have a therapeutic effect.

Drug Discovery

Lead compound identification: This involves screening vast libraries of compounds, often using high-throughput screening methods, to identify molecules that interact with the target.

Hit-to-lead optimization: Once potential hits are identified, they are chemically modified to improve their potency, selectivity, and drug-like properties. This process involves medicinal chemistry expertise.

Lead optimization: The most promising compounds undergo further optimization to enhance their efficacy, safety, and pharmacokinetic properties.

Preclinical Development

Before testing a drug in humans, extensive preclinical studies are conducted.

- In vitro studies: Compounds are tested in laboratory conditions, such as cell cultures, to assess their biological activity and potential toxicity.
- In vivo studies: Animal models are used to evaluate drug safety, efficacy, and pharmacokinetics. This stage also involves exploring different drug formulations and delivery methods.

Clinical Development

Once a compound shows promise in preclinical studies, it enters the clinical development phase, which involves testing the drug in humans.

- **Phase I:** The drug is tested on a small group of healthy volunteers to assess safety and determine the optimal dosage.
- **Phase II:** The drug is tested on a larger group of patients to evaluate its efficacy and identify side effects.
- **Phase III:** The drug is tested on a large patient population to confirm its efficacy, monitor side effects, and compare it to standard treatments.

Drug Approval and Launch

If the drug proves to be safe and effective in clinical trials, it is submitted to regulatory authorities for approval. The approval process involves rigorous review of the drug's data by regulatory agencies like the FDA (Food and Drug Administration) in the United States. Once approved, the drug can be launched into the market.

Post-Market Surveillance

Even after drug approval, ongoing monitoring is essential to detect any unexpected side effects or safety concerns. This phase is known as pharmacovigilance.

Challenges in Drug Discovery The drug discovery process is fraught with challenges, including:

- High failure rates: Most drug candidates fail in clinical trials due to lack of efficacy, safety concerns, or commercial reasons.
- Complex diseases: Many diseases have complex underlying mechanisms, making it difficult to identify suitable drug targets.
- Cost and time: Drug development is a lengthy and expensive process, requiring significant investments.
- Regulatory hurdles: Meeting regulatory requirements can be time-consuming and complex.

These challenges, advancements in technology, such as artificial intelligence, genomics, and bioinformatics, are accelerating drug discovery and development.

HEALTHCARE ANALYTICS

Healthcare analytics is the application of data analysis and statistical methods to healthcare data to extract meaningful insights and inform decision-making. It involves collecting, storing, processing, and analyzing large volumes of healthcare data, including patient records, claims data, clinical trials, and operational data.

By harnessing the power of data, healthcare organizations can:

- Identify high-risk patients, predict disease outbreaks, optimize treatment plans, and develop personalized care pathways.
- Streamline administrative processes, reduce costs, optimize resource allocation, and improve supply chain management.
- Provide evidence-based insights to inform treatment decisions, improve diagnosis accuracy, and reduce medical errors.
- Analyze clinical trial data to identify promising drug candidates and accelerate the development process.
- Identify health trends, assess the impact of public health interventions, and allocate resources effectively.

Key areas of healthcare analytics:

- Predictive analytics: Forecasting patient outcomes, identifying at-risk populations, and predicting disease outbreaks.
- Prescriptive analytics: Recommending optimal treatment plans, resource allocation, and operational strategies.
- Descriptive analytics: Summarizing past performance, identifying trends, and generating reports.
- Diagnostic analytics: Identifying the root causes of problems and opportunities for improvement.

Healthcare analytics is transforming the industry by enabling data-driven decision-making, improving patient care, and increasing operational efficiency. As technology continues to advance, we can expect to see even more innovative applications of healthcare analytics in the future.

Predictive Modeling for Patient Risk Stratification

Predictive modeling in healthcare focuses on identifying patients at high risk of developing specific diseases or experiencing adverse health events.

By analyzing vast amounts of patient data, including demographics, medical history, lifestyle factors, and genetic information, healthcare providers can build models to predict future health outcomes.

How it works:

- **Data collection:** Gathering relevant patient data from electronic health records, claims data, wearable devices, and other sources.
- **Data preprocessing:** Cleaning, transforming, and preparing data for analysis.
- **Model development:** Using statistical and machine learning techniques to build predictive models. Common algorithms include logistic regression, decision trees, random forests, and neural networks.

- **Model validation:** Assessing the model's accuracy and reliability using appropriate evaluation metrics.
- **Risk stratification:** Identifying patients at different levels of risk based on the model's predictions.

Benefits of patient risk stratification:

- Early intervention: Proactive care for high-risk patients can prevent or delay disease progression.
- Resource allocation: Optimizing the use of healthcare resources by focusing on patients with the greatest need.
- Improved patient outcomes: Early detection and intervention can lead to better health outcomes.
- Population health management: Identifying trends and patterns in disease prevalence to inform public health initiatives.

Examples of applications:

- **Chronic disease management:** Predicting the risk of heart disease, diabetes, or chronic kidney disease to enable targeted prevention and management programs.
- **Hospital readmission prevention:** Identifying patients at high risk of readmission to implement discharge planning and follow-up care.
- **Outbreak prediction:** Forecasting the spread of infectious diseases to support public health response efforts.

Predictive modeling, healthcare organizations can move from reactive to proactive care, improving patient outcomes and enhancing overall population health.

DATA SCIENCE IN FINANCE

Data science has emerged as a transformative force within the finance industry. By harnessing the power of advanced analytics and machine learning, financial institutions can extract valuable insights from vast datasets to optimize operations, mitigate risks, and uncover new opportunities. This data-driven approach is revolutionizing everything from fraud detection and risk assessment to investment strategies and customer relationship management. For instance, banks can leverage data science to identify fraudulent transactions, insurance companies can assess risk profiles more accurately, and investment firms can develop sophisticated trading algorithms.

ALGORITHMIC TRADING

Algorithmic trading, also known as algo-trading, is a method of executing orders using pre-programmed trading instructions accounting for variables such as time, price, and volume. It leverages the speed and computational power of computers to make trading decisions at a speed and frequency that is impossible for human traders. By following predefined rules and algorithms, algorithmic trading aims to remove human emotion and introduce efficiency into the trading process. This approach can be applied to a variety of trading strategies, from high-frequency trading (HFT) to more traditional strategies like arbitrage and trend following.

Algorithmic trading has become increasingly prevalent in the financial industry, with a significant portion of trading volume now executed by algorithms. While it offers potential benefits such as increased speed, reduced costs, and improved execution quality, it also raises concerns about market volatility and the potential for systemic risk.

Algorithmic Trading Works

Algorithm Development: Traders or quants develop complex algorithms based on various factors such as price, volume, time, and market conditions. These algorithms define specific trading rules and conditions.

Backtesting: The algorithm is tested on historical market data to evaluate its performance and identify potential flaws.

Execution: The algorithm is deployed on a trading platform, where it continuously monitors market data and executes trades based on the predefined rules.

Types of Algorithmic Trading Strategies

- **High-Frequency Trading (HFT):** Involves executing a large number of orders at extremely high speeds, often exploiting small price discrepancies.
- **Arbitrage:** Capitalizes on price differences between the same or similar assets across different markets.
- **Statistical Arbitrage:** Exploits statistical relationships between securities prices.
- **Mean Reversion:** Assumes that asset prices will eventually revert to their historical average.
- **Trend Following:** Identifies and capitalizes on price trends.
- **Index Arbitrage:** Exploits price discrepancies between an index and its underlying components.

Advantages of Algorithmic Trading

- Algorithms can execute trades at speeds impossible for humans.
- Removes human emotion from the trading process, reducing errors.
- Optimizes order execution and reduces transaction costs.
- Can handle large trading volumes and complex strategies.

Challenges and Risks

- Complexity: Developing and maintaining sophisticated algorithms requires specialized expertise.
- Market Impact: High-frequency trading can contribute to market volatility.
- Technological Risks: System failures or cyberattacks can lead to significant losses.
- Regulatory Challenges: The complex nature of algorithmic trading has led to increased regulatory scrutiny.

Algorithmic trading has transformed the financial industry, but it also requires careful risk management and a deep understanding of both technology and financial markets. As technology continues to advance, we can expect even more sophisticated algorithmic trading strategies to emerge.

FRAUD DETECTION

Fraud detection is the process of identifying and preventing fraudulent activities within applications, systems, and transactions.

It involves the use of various techniques and technologies to monitor transactions and customer behavior, recognizing patterns or anomalies indicative of fraudulent actions.

Types of Fraud

Fraud takes many forms, including:

- **Financial fraud:** Credit card fraud, identity theft, account takeover, and phishing.
- **Insurance fraud:** False claims, exaggerated losses, and premium fraud.
- **E-commerce fraud:** Order fraud, friendly fraud, and account takeover fraud.
- **Telecommunications fraud:** SIM swapping, caller ID spoofing, and premium rate SMS fraud.

Fraud Detection Works

Fraud detection systems typically employ a combination of techniques:

- **Rule-based systems:** Define specific conditions or patterns that trigger alerts.
- **Statistical analysis:** Identifies unusual patterns or outliers in transaction data.
- **Machine learning:** Trains models to recognize fraudulent behavior based on historical data.
- **Behavioral analytics:** Monitors customer behavior for anomalies.
- **Network analysis:** Detects suspicious relationships between accounts or entities.

Challenges in Fraud Detection

Fraudsters are constantly evolving their tactics, making it difficult to stay ahead. Challenges include:

- New fraud schemes emerge frequently.
- Balancing fraud prevention with protecting customer data.
- Incorrectly flagging legitimate transactions as fraudulent.
- Implementing and maintaining fraud detection systems can be expensive.

Benefits of Effective Fraud Detection

- Reduced financial losses: Protects businesses and consumers from financial damage.
- Improved customer experience: Minimizes fraudulent transactions and enhances customer trust.
- Enhanced brand reputation: Demonstrates a commitment to security and customer protection.
- Regulatory compliance: Helps businesses meet industry-specific regulations.

By implementing robust fraud detection measures, organizations can significantly reduce their exposure to financial losses and protect their customers.

The Role of Artificial Intelligence in Fraud Detection

Artificial Intelligence (AI) has revolutionized fraud detection by enabling systems to analyze vast amounts of data in real-time and identify complex patterns indicative of fraudulent activity.

AI is Used in Fraud Detection

Algorithms learn from historical data to identify patterns and anomalies associated with fraud. For instance, analyzing past fraudulent transactions can help models recognize similar patterns in future data.A subset of machine learning, deep learning employs neural networks to analyze complex data structures, such as images and text. This is particularly useful in detecting synthetic identities or fraudulent documents. NLP helps analyze unstructured data like social media posts, emails, and online reviews to identify potential fraud indicators. For example, detecting unusual language patterns or sentiment associated with fraudulent activities.AI can identify unusual behavior or transactions that deviate from established norms, indicating potential fraud. AI-powered systems can make rapid decisions about whether to authorize or decline transactions based on real-time data analysis.

RISK MANAGEMENT

Risk management is the systematic process of identifying, assessing, and controlling potential threats to an organization's objectives. It involves analyzing potential risks, developing strategies to mitigate them, and monitoring the effectiveness of these strategies.

Key components of risk management:

- Recognizing potential threats and vulnerabilities that could impact the organization.
- Evaluating the likelihood and potential impact of identified risks.
- Determining the severity of each risk and prioritizing them based on their potential impact.
- Developing strategies to reduce the likelihood or impact of risks.
- Continuously monitoring risks and adjusting strategies as needed.

Effective risk management is crucial for organizations of all sizes. By proactively addressing potential threats, businesses can protect their assets, reputation, and bottom line.

DATA SCIENCE IN MARKETING

Data science has revolutionized the landscape of marketing, transforming it from an art to a science. By harnessing the power of vast datasets, marketers can now gain unprecedented insights into consumer behavior, preferences, and trends. This data-driven approach enables businesses to make informed decisions, optimize marketing campaigns, and deliver personalized experiences that resonate with their target audience. From customer segmentation and acquisition to retention and loyalty, data science is driving innovation and improving marketing ROI across industries.

CUSTOMER SEGMENTATION

Customer segmentation is the process of dividing a customer base into distinct groups based on shared characteristics. By understanding these segments, businesses can tailor their marketing efforts, product offerings, and customer experiences to meet the specific needs and preferences of each group. This data-driven approach allows organizations to optimize resource allocation, increase customer satisfaction, and drive revenue growth. Through segmentation, businesses can identify high-value customers, develop targeted marketing campaigns, and create personalized customer journeys.

Customer segmentation is the process of dividing a customer base into distinct groups based on shared characteristics. It's a fundamental strategy in marketing that enables businesses to tailor their offerings and messaging to specific customer segments. By understanding the nuances of each segment, organizations can develop more effective marketing campaigns, improve customer satisfaction, and drive revenue growth.

Types of Customer Segmentation

There are several ways to segment a customer base:

- **Demographic segmentation:** Dividing customers based on factors like age, gender, income, education, occupation, and family size.
- **Geographic segmentation:** Grouping customers based on location, region, city, or country.
- **Psychographic segmentation:** Categorizing customers based on their values, lifestyles, interests, and personality traits.
- **Behavioral segmentation:** Grouping customers based on their purchasing behavior, usage patterns, and loyalty.

- **Needs-based segmentation**: Segmenting customers based on their specific needs and desired benefits.

The Benefits of Customer Segmentation

- Improved targeting: Delivering more relevant messages to specific customer groups.
- Increased customer satisfaction: Meeting the unique needs of different customer segments.
- Enhanced customer loyalty: Building stronger relationships with loyal customers.
- Optimized marketing spend: Allocating resources effectively to target high-value segments.
- Product development: Identifying new product opportunities based on customer needs.

Implementing Customer Segmentation

1. **Define segmentation goals**: Clearly outline the objectives of the segmentation process.
2. **Collect customer data**: Gather relevant data points, such as demographics, purchase history, and website behavior.
3. **Choose segmentation variables**: Select the most appropriate variables based on your goals.
4. **Analyze customer data**: Use statistical methods and data mining techniques to identify distinct segments.
5. **Create customer profiles**: Develop detailed profiles of each customer segment, including their characteristics, needs, and preferences.
6. **Develop targeted marketing campaigns**: Create customized marketing messages and channels for each segment.

By effectively implementing customer segmentation, businesses can gain a competitive advantage and achieve long-term success.

RECOMMENDATION SYSTEMS

Recommendation systems are algorithms that suggest items to users based on their preferences and past behavior. These systems have become ubiquitous in various industries, from e-commerce to entertainment, and play a crucial role in enhancing user experience and driving engagement.

By analyzing vast amounts of data, recommendation systems can predict the items or content a user is likely to enjoy, leading to increased customer satisfaction and loyalty. They are powered by a combination of techniques, including collaborative filtering, content-based filtering, and hybrid approaches.

Key components of recommendation systems:

- Gathering information about users, items, and their interactions.
- Cleaning and preparing data for analysis.
- Identifying relevant features or attributes of users and items.
- Developing algorithms to predict user preferences.
- Providing personalized recommendations based on the model's output.
- Measuring the performance of the recommendation system.

Recommendation systems have a profound impact on user behavior and business outcomes. By effectively leveraging these systems, companies can increase sales, improve customer retention, and enhance overall user experience.

MARKETING AUTOMATION

Marketing automation is essentially software that handles repetitive marketing tasks without human intervention. Think of it as your digital assistant, tirelessly working to nurture leads, engage customers, and drive sales.

How Does It Work?

Marketing automation involves:

- Gathering information about your audience, their behavior, and preferences.

- Dividing your audience into groups based on shared characteristics.
- Designing automated sequences of actions triggered by specific events or behaviors.
- Delivering personalized content and offers across various channels (email, social media, SMS, etc.).
- Tracking and measuring campaign effectiveness to optimize future efforts.

Benefits of Marketing Automation

- Automating repetitive tasks frees up your team to focus on strategic initiatives.
- Deliver personalized content at the right time to move leads through the sales funnel.
- Build stronger relationships through targeted and timely interactions.
- Gain valuable insights into customer behavior to optimize campaigns.
- Measure the impact of your marketing efforts and allocate resources effectively.

Common Use Cases

- **Email Marketing:** Send targeted emails based on user behavior, preferences, and lifecycle stage.
- **Lead Scoring:** Assign values to leads based on their actions and interactions.
- **Social Media Management:** Schedule posts, engage with followers, and analyze performance.
- **CRM Integration:** Sync customer data for a unified view of the customer journey.
- **Sales Enablement:** Provide sales teams with the right information at the right time.

Key Features to Look For in Marketing Automation Software

- Robust features for creating, sending, and analyzing email campaigns.
- Tools for capturing, nurturing, and scoring leads.
- Seamless connection with your customer relationship management system.
- Comprehensive data insights to measure campaign performance.
- Flexible options for creating complex automated processes.

In essence, marketing automation is a powerful tool that can help businesses streamline operations, improve customer experiences, and drive growth

DATA SCIENCE IN OTHER INDUSTRIES

Data science has emerged as a transformative force, revolutionizing industries far beyond the realm of technology. Its ability to extract meaningful insights from vast datasets has unlocked unprecedented opportunities across sectors. From healthcare to finance, retail to manufacturing, organizations are harnessing the power of data to optimize operations, enhance customer experiences, and drive innovation

Manufacturing

Data science is reshaping the manufacturing landscape. By analyzing data from sensors, machines, and production processes, manufacturers can optimize operations, predict equipment failures, and enhance product quality. Predictive maintenance, for instance, uses data to forecast when machinery is likely to break down, allowing for proactive repairs and preventing costly downtime. Additionally, data-driven insights can streamline supply chain management, reduce waste, and improve overall efficiency.

Retail

In the retail industry, data science is revolutionizing customer experiences and driving sales. Retailers leverage customer data to personalize recommendations, optimize pricing, and enhance marketing campaigns. For example, by analyzing purchase history and browsing behavior, retailers can offer tailored product suggestions. Furthermore, data-driven insights can optimize inventory management, prevent stockouts, and reduce markdowns.

Energy

The energy sector is undergoing a significant transformation, driven by data science. From renewable energy sources to traditional power generation, data is essential for optimizing operations, improving grid efficiency, and enabling the transition to a sustainable future. For instance, analyzing weather data and energy consumption patterns can help utilities predict demand and optimize energy distribution. Additionally, data-driven insights can accelerate the development of new energy technologies and improve energy efficiency.

Transportation

Data science is transforming the transportation industry by improving efficiency, safety, and sustainability. By analyzing data from vehicles, traffic patterns, and passenger behavior, transportation companies can optimize routes, reduce congestion, and enhance the overall travel experience. For example, predictive maintenance can be used to prevent vehicle breakdowns, while real-time traffic data can help optimize delivery routes. Additionally, data-driven insights can inform the development of autonomous vehicles and smart cities.

These are just a few examples of how data science is being applied across different industries. The potential applications are vast and continue to expand as data becomes more accessible and sophisticated analytics tools emerge.

SEVEN

THE FUTURE OF DATA SCIENCE

The future of data science is a landscape of boundless potential, marked by rapid technological advancements and an insatiable appetite for data-driven insights. As the volume and complexity of data continue to explode, data scientists will play an increasingly pivotal role in shaping industries and societies. From artificial intelligence and machine learning to quantum computing and data ethics, the field is poised for unprecedented growth and innovation.The future of data science is poised to be even more transformative, with advancements in artificial intelligence and machine learning pushing the boundaries of what's possible. As data continues to grow exponentially, data scientists will be at the forefront of developing sophisticated models capable of uncovering intricate patterns and making increasingly accurate predictions. The integration of data science with other disciplines, such as biology, physics, and social sciences, will lead to groundbreaking discoveries and innovations. Moreover, ethical considerations will become paramount as data scientists grapple with issues of privacy, bias, and the responsible use of data.

The scientist of the future is a visionary equipped with an arsenal of knowledge and technological prowess. They are not merely researchers confined to laboratories, but global citizens grappling with complex challenges that demand innovative solutions. Their work will transcend disciplinary boundaries, merging the humanities with the sciences to create a harmonious coexistence between humanity and technology. Armed with artificial intelligence as a collaborator, the scientist of tomorrow will explore uncharted territories, pushing the frontiers of human understanding and shaping a sustainable future for generations to come.

Skillset Requirements for the Scientist of the Future

The scientist of tomorrow will require a unique blend of hard and soft skills. Beyond the traditional scientific acumen, they must be adept at:

- Computational Thinking: Proficiency in programming, data analysis, and machine learning will be essential to harness the power of big data and AI.
- Interdisciplinary Knowledge: A deep understanding of multiple fields, such as biology, physics, chemistry, and computer science, will be crucial for tackling complex problems.
- Creativity and Innovation: The ability to think outside the box and develop novel solutions will be paramount in driving scientific progress.
- Communication and Collaboration: Effective communication skills are essential for disseminating research findings, collaborating with diverse teams, and engaging with the public.
- Ethical Reasoning: A strong ethical compass will guide decision-making in areas such as data privacy, AI bias, and the responsible use of technology.

Moreover, adaptability and a lifelong learning mindset will be crucial as the scientific landscape rapidly evolves.

Career Paths for the Scientist of the Future

The career paths for future scientists will be diverse and dynamic. Traditional academic roles will continue to exist, but new opportunities will emerge at the intersection of science and technology. Some potential career paths include:

- AI Research Scientist: Developing advanced algorithms and models to solve complex problems.
- Data Scientist: Extracting insights from vast datasets to inform decision-making.
- Biotechnologist: Creating innovative solutions in healthcare, agriculture, and environmental science.
- Climate Scientist: Developing strategies to mitigate climate change and build resilience.
- Space Scientist: Exploring the universe and developing technologies for space exploration.
- Entrepreneur: Commercializing scientific discoveries and creating new ventures.
- Policy Maker: Using scientific evidence to inform public policy and shape societal outcomes.

It's important to note that these roles are likely to evolve as technology advances and societal needs change.

Ethical Considerations for the Scientist of the Future

As scientific knowledge and technology progress, ethical considerations become increasingly complex. Future scientists will need to grapple with issues such as:

- Data Privacy: Protecting sensitive information while harnessing the power of data.
- AI Bias: Ensuring that AI systems are fair and unbiased.
- Bioethics: Addressing ethical implications of advancements in biotechnology, such as gene editing.
- Environmental Impact: Minimizing the environmental footprint of scientific research and development.
- Social Responsibility: Considering the broader societal implications of scientific breakthroughs.

Scientists will have a crucial role in shaping the ethical framework for future technologies. Collaboration with ethicists, policymakers, and the public will be essential to navigate these complex challenges.

The intersection of data science and society is poised to redefine the world as we know it. As data continues to proliferate and computational power grows exponentially, data science is emerging as a driving force for innovation and progress. Its impact will be felt across every sector, from healthcare and education to finance and government. However, with great power comes great responsibility, and ensuring that data is used ethically and equitably will be a critical challenge for the years to come

Impact of Data Science on Jobs

The rise of data science is reshaping the job market. On one hand, it's creating a surge of new roles, from data scientists and analysts to machine learning engineers and data architects. These roles are in high demand across industries, driving economic growth and innovation.

On the other hand, automation driven by data science and AI is also transforming existing jobs, potentially leading to job displacement in certain sectors. However, it's essential to note that while automation may eliminate some routine tasks, it often creates new opportunities for higher-skilled roles. The key to navigating this changing landscape is a focus on continuous learning and upskilling to adapt to evolving job requirements.

Privacy Concerns in Data Science

The abundance of data collected and analyzed in data science raises significant privacy concerns. With every click, purchase, or social media interaction, individuals leave digital footprints that can be potentially exploited. This has led to increased scrutiny on data collection, storage, and usage practices.

Regulations like GDPR and CCPA have been implemented to protect individuals' rights and hold organizations accountable. Data scientists must prioritize data privacy by implementing robust security measures, anonymizing data where possible, and obtaining explicit consent when necessary. Striking a balance between data utilization and privacy protection is crucial for building trust.

Social Responsibility in Data Science

Data science has the potential to address some of the world's most pressing challenges, but it can also exacerbate existing inequalities if not used responsibly. Data scientists have a responsibility to ensure that their work benefits society as a whole.

This includes addressing biases in data and algorithms, preventing discriminatory outcomes, and using data to promote social good. For instance, data science can be employed to improve healthcare access, reduce poverty, and combat climate change. However, it's essential to be mindful of the potential negative impacts and to mitigate them through ethical practices. By prioritizing social responsibility, data scientists can contribute to a more equitable and sustainable future.

EIGHT
CONCLUSION

The future of data science is a dynamic landscape characterized by rapid technological advancement and evolving societal needs. As data continues to grow exponentially, so too will the demand for skilled professionals who can harness its power to drive innovation and solve complex problems. Emerging technologies like artificial intelligence, machine learning, and the Internet of Things will further propel data science forward, creating new opportunities and challenges. The ethical implications of data usage will remain paramount, requiring a strong emphasis on responsible data practices. Ultimately, the success of data science will hinge on its ability to deliver tangible benefits to society while upholding the highest standards of privacy and fairness. The trajectory of data science is marked by rapid evolution, driven by technological advancements and the increasing volume and complexity of data. Several key trends will shape the field in the coming years The integration of AI and machine learning will be pivotal. These technologies will enhance data analysis, automation, and predictive modeling. Advancements in natural language processing and computer vision will enable data scientists to extract insights from unstructured data sources like text, images, and videos. The exponential growth of data necessitates robust infrastructure. Cloud computing will continue to be a cornerstone, providing scalable and cost-effective solutions for data storage, processing, and analysis. Distributed computing frameworks will become increasingly important for handling massive datasets. The proliferation of IoT devices will generate vast amounts of data. Data scientists will play a crucial role in extracting valuable insights from this data to optimize processes, enhance decision-making, and develop new products and services. As data becomes more central to society, privacy and ethical considerations will intensify. Data scientists will need to adhere to stringent regulations, develop robust data protection measures, and ensure fair and unbiased algorithms. There is a growing trend towards democratizing data science, making it accessible to a broader audience. This includes the development of user-friendly tools and platforms, as well as educational initiatives to equip more people with data literacy skills.

These trends will collectively drive the evolution of data science, creating new opportunities and challenges for practitioners. By staying abreast of these developments and acquiring the necessary skills, data scientists can position themselves at the forefront of innovation and make significant contributions to society.

The rapid growth of data science has brought forth a myriad of challenges that require careful consideration. These challenges range from technical hurdles to ethical dilemmas. Data quality is a cornerstone of effective data science. Poor quality data can lead to inaccurate insights, flawed models, and ultimately, poor decision-making. Variations in data formats, definitions, and standards can hinder analysis. Errors and inaccuracies in data can skew results and undermine confidence in findings. Missing data points can limit the scope of analysis and impact model performance. Ensuring that data is aligned with specific business objectives is crucial.

Overcoming these challenges requires a multifaceted approach, including data cleaning, validation, and enrichment processes. Additionally, implementing robust data governance practices and establishing clear data quality metrics is essential to maintain data integrity over time.

www.ingramcontent.com/pod-product-compliance
Lightning Source LLC
Chambersburg PA
CBHW031430130726
47989CB00003B/1074